Playing Small

Jenn Noble-Beninger

This book is intended for informational and educational purposes only. The author shares insights and experiences to support your personal growth; however, results will vary based on individual effort and circumstances. The reader assumes full responsibility for their actions and decisions.

ISBN: 979-8-234-10610-0

For my daughters, Isabella and Avalon. My greatest adventure. My greatest love.

And to every person who still thinks they have to play small, this one is for you. You don't. You never did. Your genius has been in there the whole time, waiting for you to stop standing in its way. I wrote this book to show you, this is the way. Now stop waiting and go read it.

Acknowledgments

To Isabella and Avalon —

Isabella, you are my oldest, my first, my forever person. You were my girl before any of this existed, and you will be my girl long after the last page turns. You have a heart so big and so kind it stops people in their tracks. You love without holding back, think without limits, and see patterns in people that others miss entirely. Watching you work is watching someone who was born to do exactly this. You walk into a room, and people feel it. You have no fear, no ceiling, no version of yourself that plays small, and that alone makes you one of the most extraordinary humans I have ever known. You are not just my daughter. You are unstoppable. You are brilliant. You are the kind of woman who does not just change her own life, you walk into other people's lives and changes those too. The world has no idea what is coming. I do. I have always known. Your genius has always been blinding, and I could not be more in awe of who you are becoming.

Michael, thank you for loving my daughter the way she deserves to be loved. You showed up steady and kind when it mattered most, and you have never wavered. Your patience, your humor, and the quiet way you support Isabella in everything she does have not gone unnoticed. She shines brightest because you are besides her, and I will always be grateful that she gets to walk through this life with someone who truly sees her. I could not have hand-picked anyone more right for her if I tried.

Avalon, there's a fire in you wrapped in the softest, most generous heart I have ever known. From the moment you arrived, you wrapped yourself around my heart and never let go. You see the good in people before they see it in themselves, love without keeping score, and give without ever being asked. You are funny in the way that sneaks up on you, the kind of funny that makes everything lighter and everyone feel at home. You have a servant's heart and a warrior's spirit, and somehow you make both look like the most natural thing in the world. While I was busy changing the world, you were holding it steady at home, cooking the meals I will never cook (we are all genuinely grateful), and loving me with a fullness that takes my breath away. You aren't just my daughter. You are my heart. You are my light. You're going to set this world on fire in the most beautiful way, and I will be cheering the loudest when you do.

To my Dad Tim, my Mom Linda and my Brother Ryan,

Dad, you have always shown up for me every single time, in every season, without fail. No questions asked, no hesitation, ever. Your jokes were so corny they should have come with butter, and I laughed every single time anyway. You are the kind of person who makes everything feel possible just by being in the room.

Mom, your love has never had conditions. It has never come with fine print or an expiration date. It has simply always been there, unwavering, unshakeable, the kind of love that makes a person feel like they can do anything. You held space for my genius long before I knew I had any, and you never once stopped believing it was there.

Ryan, my partner in crime, my ride-or-die since before I had any idea what I was doing. Nobody has made me laugh harder, gotten into more trouble with me, or known me longer. You are woven into who I am in ways I can't fully explain and wouldn't trade for anything. Not even the questionable decisions. Those are my favorite.

You are all the roots beneath everything I have ever grown.

This book would not exist without two people who refused to let it stay a dream.

Jessica Lehnes, you are not just a collaborator. You are not just the woman who got this book started. You are family. You are the friend who shows up, who asks the hard questions, who sits across from you and says *I see you, now let's go.* You were the instigator, the interviewer, the one who refused to let this stay locked inside me. You saw the book before there was a book. Without you, this book would still be a beautiful dream I hadn't found the courage to chase. I love you for all of it.

Isabella, you brought it home. You edited it, you finished it, you pushed it across the finish line when I had nothing left. The book everyone is holding exists because you would *not* let it *not* exist.

To Angel Tuccy and her incredible team, you were the structure when things felt shapeless and the loudest cheer when things felt impossible. You held the vision of this book with a fierceness I will never forget and made sure every single detail landed exactly where it needed to. Thank you for never giving up on this, or on me.

To my entire Genius Unlocked team, you show up every single day with your whole hearts, holding space for other people's genius while quietly championing mine. This book is yours too. All of it.

To my mentors and trainers, you lifted me up so I could finally see the ripple I was making. It was something that you had seen all along. You held me to the highest standard, never let me fall back into old patterns, and believed in me through it all.

To my clients, you trusted me with the most sacred thing a person can hand over: their own transformation. You did the work. You showed up. You cracked yourselves open and chose to grow. I thought I was only your teacher. The truth is, you were mine too. Every single one of you lives in these pages, whether you know it or not. Thank you for that gift.

P.S. If I forgot to mention you by name, I promise it was human error and not personal. Find me, remind me, and I owe you champagne. The good kind.

CONTENTS

FOREWORD

There are books you read… and then there are books that read *you.* *F Playing Small* by Jenn Noble-Beninger is the latter.

From the very first pages, I knew this wasn't just another personal development book filled with good ideas and surface-level motivation. This is a call forward. A disruption. A mirror. And if you let it, it will be a turning point. Because the truth is, *the world has enough mediocre people playing it safe and staying small.*

What the world needs—what it has always needed—is YOU.
At full volume.
At full power.

Taking up every inch of space you deserve… and then some. In my work with leaders, authors, and visionaries across the globe, I see it all the time: brilliant, capable, deeply called individuals holding themselves back. Not because they lack talent or opportunity—because somewhere along the way, they were conditioned to shrink. To fit. To filter. To perform a version of themselves that felt acceptable instead of authentic. Jenn dismantles that conditioning with precision and power.

She reminds us of something we may have forgotten: You were not born for mediocrity. You were not born to spend your life managing the surface of things, running old programs that were never yours to begin with, vibrating at frequencies installed by people who were doing their own version of the same thing.

You were not born to play small or stay quiet or make yourself easier to be around at the expense of being fully yourself. You were born for this.

This book doesn't just inspire you, it invites you into a deeper level of personal responsibility and possibility. It asks you to stop skimming the surface of your abilities and instead go inward… to the place where real transformation lives. Because this is where the real work begins.

This book will be the beginning of a conversation. And not just any conversation, the most important one you will ever have with the deepest levels of your own unconscious mind. With proper support. At the depth where the patterns actually live… And where everything you have ever wanted is patiently, absolutely, definitely waiting.

I can say with full conviction: this is my new favorite book. It's one I will be recommending to my friends, my clients, and every person who tells me they're ready to elevate their life and finally step into the version of themselves they know they are meant to be.

If you're holding this book in your hands, consider it confirmation.
You're ready.

And the version of you that's been waiting? She's not playing small anymore.

— Angel Tuccy, author of Author-licity

CHAPTER 1
The Genius You Were Born to Be

"You will always be too much of something for someone: too big, too loud, too soft, too edgy. If you round out your edges, you lose your edge."
— Danielle LaPorte

The day I was born, I was already inconvenient; late, loud, and completely unapologetic, arriving on my mother's 23rd birthday like I owned the place. That should have been everyone's first clue that some things never change.

My mom and I are complete opposites; she's the calm to my storm, the quiet to my loud. And if you've ever loved someone who is fundamentally nothing like you, you know that kind of relationship has its own beautiful chaos. She'd be the first to laugh and say, "I never knew how to handle Jenn. She was always too much." And honestly? She wasn't wrong. I was a lot. I still am.

Too loud. Too opinionated. Too much energy. Too much everything.

Sound familiar?

Somewhere along the way, someone convinced you that being "too much" of something was a problem.

Maybe it was a parent who didn't know how to handle your energy. Maybe it was a teacher who preferred quiet, compliant students. Maybe it was a society that taught you that taking up space was selfish, that having big dreams was unrealistic, that speaking up meant you were being rude.

Same Kid, Completely Different World

I had two very different sets of grandparents, and they taught me everything I needed to know about how other people's filters distort the truth about who you are.

My dad's parents thought I was amazing. My grandmother treated me like I was the cream of the crop, the best thing that could have happened. She wanted to give me the world. When I was with her, I felt like a genius. I felt like I could do anything, be anything, create anything.

My mom's parents were the complete opposite. I loved them, and their rulebook was clear: children were seen and not heard, opinions were not welcome, and the dinner table was not a democracy. Naturally, I got sent away from it…a lot!

Same kid. Same energy. Same genius. Completely different experience.

Here's the kicker: I wasn't different when I was at my dad's parents' house versus my mom's parents' house. I was the same "too much" kid in both places. The only thing that changed was how the adults around me chose to see me.

One set of grandparents saw my energy as a gift. The other saw it as a problem to be managed.

And that's when I learned one of the most important lessons of my life: Other people's discomfort with your energy has absolutely nothing to do with whether or not you're a genius. It has everything to do with their own limitations, their own fears, their own programming about what's acceptable and what's not.

The Genius Signs You Missed

You know what happens when you spend your childhood learning to make yourself smaller? You start believing that small is your natural size. You start thinking that your big energy, your wild dreams, your audacious goals are somehow wrong, inappropriate, or "too much."

And here's what I've learned after working with thousands of people: The things you got in trouble for as a kid are often your greatest gifts in disguise.

Take me, for example. When I was in Girl Scouts, I became obsessed with selling cookies. Not just selling them, I wanted to dominate the cookie sales game. Every single year, I was the top seller in our entire town, across all troops. I won every award they had.

Back then, you had to go door to door with an order form. People would sign it, and then you'd have to go back weeks later to deliver the cookies. I was eight years old, trudging through Colorado snow, knocking on strangers' doors, convincing them to buy cookies they wouldn't get for another month.

What did the adults around me say about this? "Jennifer's so competitive." "She's so driven." "She never knows when to quit." All said with exasperation, like these were character flaws I needed to outgrow.

And think about what I was actually doing: I was building relationships with strangers. I was following up on commitments. I was learning to handle rejection (because not everyone said yes). I was managing inventory, tracking orders, and delivering on promises. I was eight years old and running my own business.

That wasn't a character flaw. That was my entrepreneurial genius showing up.

The same energy that made adults tired was the same energy that made me successful. The same determination that made teachers say I was "too much" was the same determination that would later help me build a 7-figure business.

Your "too much" isn't a bug in your system. It's a feature.

Think about your own childhood. What did you get in trouble for? What did people say you needed to tone down or control? What came so naturally to you that adults found it exhausting?

- Were you too curious? That's research and innovation skills.
- Were you too talkative? That's communication and connection abilities.
- Were you too stubborn? That's determination and persistence.
- Were you too sensitive? That's emotional intelligence and empathy.
- Were you too dramatic? That's storytelling and influence capabilities.

Society has this backwards idea that children should be convenient for adults. If a kid's natural energy, interests, or way of being creates any inconvenience for the grown-ups around them, the kid gets labeled as having a problem that needs to be fixed.

What if the problem isn't with the kid? What if the problem is with a system that wants to turn naturally genius children into compliant, manageable adults?

What Playing Small Actually Costs You

Here's what nobody tells you about playing small: it's expensive as hell.

I don't just mean financially, although it definitely costs you money. I mean, it costs you everything: your dreams, your relationships, your health, your sanity, and your joy.

Let me tell you about the price I paid for learning to shrink myself.

My family moved constantly when I was growing up. California to Colorado to New York and back to California. Every time we moved, I had to figure out what version of myself was acceptable in this new place. I became a master at reading rooms and adjusting my energy accordingly.

In Colorado, I kept to myself because being the new kid is its own special kind of brutal. New York taught me something Colorado never did: that I could become so invisible I didn't even have a name anymore. I became "Colorado." Not Jennifer. Not Jenn. “Colorado.” Not my name - my zip code. And seventh graders — God, seventh graders are ruthless — they ran with it. I learned real fast to take up as little space as possible. To be seen even less than I already was.

And then we moved back to California, where I was handed a brand new label before I even unpacked my boxes: I had an "attitude." I was "intense." I was "a lot." I hadn't earned it. I just wasn't one of them, hadn't grown up with them, didn't know their history, hadn't put in the years required to belong. High schoolers don't extend grace to outsiders. They close ranks. And I was always on the outside of those ranks, the perpetual new kid who was too New York for California and too Colorado for New York and too California for anywhere else. So I stopped trying to fit in and started trying to disappear instead.

Each move required me to shrink a little bit more. I put limits on myself to try to stay safe and protected. I had to figure out what people wanted me to be in each new place, and then I had to contort myself to fit into that box.

By the time I graduated high school, I had no idea who I actually was. I only knew who I needed to be to avoid getting picked on, criticized, or rejected. And that pattern followed me into adulthood.

I would scan every room I entered to figure out what version of myself would be most acceptable. I would tone down my excitement so I didn’t seem “too much.” I would minimize my successes, so I didn’t seem threatening. I would shrink my dreams so they seemed more “realistic.”

Do you know what that kind of constant shape-shifting does to a person? It’s exhausting. You lose track of your own desires because you’re so busy managing other people's comfort levels. You start making decisions based on what you think you should want instead of what you actually want. You become a stranger to yourself.

And then you wonder why you feel stuck, why you're not happy, why your life doesn't feel like it's yours.

It's because you've been living someone else's version of your life.

Playing small doesn't just limit your possibilities. It suffocates your soul.

I see this all the time in my work. High achievers who look successful on the outside and feel empty on the inside. People who have everything they thought they wanted and still feel like something's missing. Entrepreneurs who hit their goals and feel like frauds. Parents who give everything to their kids and lose themselves in the process.

They're all living smaller versions of themselves, and they can feel the gap between who they are and who they're capable of becoming.

That gap? That's the cost of playing small.

The Science of Why You're Here

Let's get nerdy for a minute, because I want you to understand just how miraculous your existence actually is. And I mean that literally…with math.

In order for you to exist, you had to beat out millions of other sperm to get here. And that isn't a coincidence. You didn't accidentally win the greatest race of your life. You were meant to be here. You were divinely created, and you sure as hell weren't divinely created for lack and scarcity.

Think about it. What are the odds? Scientists estimate that at the moment of conception, there are 200 to 300 million sperm racing toward a single egg. And out of all those millions, YOU were the one. You fought your way through, you persevered, you WON. You are literally a fucking winner from the moment you were conceived.

Now, let's zoom out even further.

The odds of your parents meeting? Approximately 1 in 20,000.

The odds of them staying together long enough to have you? About 1 in 2,000.

The odds of the right sperm meeting the right egg at exactly the right time? 1 in 400 trillion.

But wait, there's more…

The odds of all your ancestors going back thousands of generations, surviving long enough to reproduce? The odds of every single one of them meeting their mate, having children, and those children surviving to reproductive age?

The number is so large that mathematicians basically call it impossible. One scientist calculated it as 1 in 10, followed by 2.5 million zeros. To put that in perspective, there is no scale large enough to hold that number. No analogy that does it justice. The universe has been around for 13.8 billion years and has never once produced another you.

And yet, here you are!

It gets even better. You're not just here during any random time in history. You're here during the most incredible period of human existence. You have access to more information than any library in the history of the world. You can connect with people across the globe instantly. You can learn any skill, start any business, create any life you want.

You're also here at a time when the universe itself is expanding. Here's the wild part: as consciousness grows, as humans evolve, as we become more of who we're capable of being, the actual fabric of reality stretches to accommodate our growth.

Think about that. The universe is literally growing because *you're* growing.

And you're worried about being too much?

Here's what I know about human evolution: We're not done yet. We're not the finished product. The human brain is still developing, still adding new capabilities. You have a brain that's specifically wired for genius-level thinking, and you're using it to worry about whether you're too much for people who are committed to being too little.

We weren't put on this planet just to survive. Animals survive. Humans are capable of creating, innovating, loving, building, healing, and transforming not just their own lives, but the lives of everyone around them.

You have access to parts of your brain that are specifically designed for expansion, creation, and possibility. Using those extraordinary capabilities to limit yourself is like buying a Ferrari and only driving it in first gear.

Stop it!

YOUR FIRST GENIUS ASSIGNMENT

You've been nodding along this whole chapter, thinking "yes, that's me." I know. I also know you'd rather keep reading than actually do the work. But reading about change doesn't create it. This does. So pick up your pen.

Wait! Before you read another word, go download your workbook **by scanning the QR code below and print that thing out.**

This book is not a museum piece; you do not rope it off, admire it, and walk away unchanged. The assignments are where the transformation actually lives, and skipping them is the personal development equivalent of reading a cookbook and wondering why you're still hungry. Fill in the lines, scribble in the margins, make it yours. Pen and paper only, writing by hand bypasses your brain's filter and goes straight to the good stuff. Set aside 15–20 minutes somewhere quiet. Then come back. We've got work to do.

You will find the following pages correspond to pages in your workbook. Use your workbook to do the writing and still follow along here in the book.

STEP 1: FIND YOUR "TOO MUCH"

Think back to your childhood. What's one thing you consistently got in trouble for, criticized for, or told to "tone down"? (i.e.: too loud, too dramatic, too stubborn, too sensitive, too curious, too intense, too needy, too emotional, too weird, too unrealistic, too unpredictable)

STEP 2: REFRAME IT AS YOUR SUPERPOWER

Now I want you to reframe that "flaw" as a superpower.

If you were "too loud," own it —
that's natural leadership and communication that commands a room.
If you were "too dramatic," own it —
that's storytelling and influence that moves people to action.
If you were "too stubborn," own it —
that's determination that doesn't quit when everyone else does.
If you were "too sensitive," own it —
that's emotional intelligence at a level most people will never access.
If you were "too curious," own it —
that's a mind that refuses to accept the surface when there's so much more underneath.
If you were "too intense," own it —
that's focus and passion that creates things most people only dream about.
If you were "too needy," own it —
that's a deep capacity for connection and love that the world desperately needs more of.
If you were "too emotional," own it —
that's empathy and depth that makes you someone people actually feel safe with.
If you were "too weird," own it —
that's originality and creative genius that can't be replicated or manufactured.
If you were "too unrealistic," own it —
that's vision that refuses to be limited by what already exists.
If you were "too unpredictable," own it —
that's someone who can't be contained by other people's small expectations.

STEP 3: IMAGINE BEING CELEBRATED FOR IT

How might your life be different if you had been celebrated for this trait instead of criticized for it?

Your business — Would you have started sooner? Charged more from day one? Stopped waiting until you felt "ready" and just built the thing you knew you were meant to build?

Your relationships — Would you have stopped settling for people who needed you small? Attracted partners, friends, and collaborators who actually celebrated the real you instead of the edited version?

Your confidence — Would you have walked into every room knowing you belonged there? Stopped rehearsing your worth and just lived it?

Your willingness to take risks — Would you have bet on yourself earlier? Said yes to the things that terrified you instead of talking yourself out of them with a hundred unreasonable excuses?

Your pursuit of big dreams — Would you have stopped calling your vision "unrealistic" and started calling it inevitable? Would you have permitted yourself to want what you actually want, out loud, without apology?

Your voice — Would you have spoken up sooner? Shared your ideas without second-guessing yourself? Stopped shrinking in rooms where you deserved to take up space?

Your money — Would you have charged more, asked for more, believed you deserved more sooner?

Your creativity — Would you have created without permission? Shared your ideas without waiting for someone to validate them first?

Your leadership — Would you have stepped into rooms and led instead of waiting to be invited?

Your dreams — Would you have gone bigger, faster, without the years of talking yourself out of what you actually wanted?

Your identity — Would you have known earlier who you actually were instead of spending years becoming who everyone else needed you to be?

Your joy — Would you have let yourself be fully, unapologetically happy without waiting for it to be taken away?

STEP 4: UNLOCK WHAT'S POSSIBLE RIGHT NOW

What would be possible in your life right now if you stopped justifying this trait and started leveraging it instead?

And don't answer this in generalities. Not "I'd be more successful" or "I'd be happier." Get specific. What would you actually do? What would you stop tolerating? What would you finally say yes to, and what would you say hell no to?

If you woke up tomorrow and fully owned this trait as your superpower, what's the first thing you'd do differently? What meeting would you show up to differently? What conversation would you finally have? What would you stop apologizing for?

Now here's the one that really matters: what has justifying and tolerating other people's discomfort with this trait, instead of owning it, already cost you? In time, money, relationships, opportunities, joy, what's the real price tag of **playing small with your own genius?**

Sit with that for a minute. Really sit with it. Use your workbook.

This isn't just a cute exercise. This is the beginning of everything. You cannot step into your genius until you stop apologizing for the very things that make you a genius.

The world doesn't need you to be smaller, quieter, more manageable, or more convenient. The world needs you to be more you, more of whatever it is that makes you uniquely capable of creating, contributing, and making a difference.

So here's what we're going to do together in this book: we're going to clean off all the dirty filters that have been distorting your view of yourself. We're going to identify all the ways you've been programmed to play small. We're going to bring awareness to the unconscious patterns that have been running your life, and we're going to give you the tools to start shifting them.

This isn't about me waving a magic wand and fixing you, because you're not broken. This is about you learning to see yourself clearly, understanding how your mind actually works, and making conscious choices about who you want to become.

Some of these shifts will happen quickly. Others will take time and practice. All of them will require your willingness to look at yourself with fresh eyes and question the stories you've been telling yourself about what's possible.

Because you, my friend, are not an accident. You are not a mistake. You are not too much.

You are exactly the right amount of everything the world needs right now.

The question isn't whether you're a genius. The question is: Are you ready to start believing it?

CHAPTER 2
THE STORIES WE TELL OURSELVES

"We are the stories we tell ourselves. The most important conversation is the one you have with yourself."
— Colin O'Brady

The story you're telling yourself about your life is probably complete bullshit.

That's the best news you'll hear all day.

Because if it's bullshit, that means you don't have to believe it anymore, and you can change it. And changing your story? That's literally how you change your life.

First, let me blow your mind with something most people never realize: You're not living in reality. You're living in a story about reality. And that story is being written by a part of your brain that's more concerned with keeping you alive than helping you thrive.

Buckle up, buttercup. We're about to take a deep dive into the story factory between your ears, and what you discover might piss you off.

Good.

Anger means you're ready to do something about it.

The Great Story Scam

Here's what nobody told you growing up: your brain is lying to you. Not maliciously, it's just wired to make meaning out of everything, whether that meaning is true or not. And it does this so fast, so automatically, that by the time you think you're seeing reality, you're actually seeing your brain's very confident, very flawed interpretation of it. Your brain doesn't detect truth; it manufactures it. It takes everything that happens, runs it through years of filters, fears, and old programming, and hands you back a story labeled "reality." Spoiler alert: *it's not.*

Every single day, your brain is writing stories about your experiences, your capabilities, your worth, your future, and what's possible for someone like you. And you've been walking around thinking these stories are facts.

They're not facts. They're interpretations. And most of them are outdated, inherited, or just plain wrong.

Let me show you exactly how this works, not in theory, in my actual life.

After I had barely graduated high school, I took a gap year. Simple enough, right? Except my brain didn't file it as "gap year." My brain filed it as evidence. Evidence that I wasn't smart enough for college. That I needed extra time because I couldn't keep up. That maybe college wasn't for someone like me.

One decision. One story. And just like that, my brain had a new filter, and it was going to spend the next several years proving that filter right.

So there I was, working two jobs. Soul-sucking, genius-draining, clock-watching jobs that paid $8 an hour. And you know what the terrifying part was? Part of me had already accepted that this was it. Who do I think I am to want something bigger? That $8 an hour was the ceiling. That this was what someone like me, someone who needed a gap year, someone who maybe wasn't quite smart enough, could amount to.

I didn't know it at the time that it was my unconscious filters running the show.

Then I met Eric.

Eric was a cop. Solid guy. Very clear on what he wanted. What he wanted was a wife who stayed home, cooked, and cleaned. (I have not cooked a real meal since 1997, and my house cleaner is basically my longest relationship). Somewhere in the fog of $8-an-hour exhaustion and "maybe I'm not smart enough," I almost let that become my story too.

When I told him I was thinking about college, he took me on a cruise. A whole ass cruise. The man literally put me on a boat in the middle of the ocean to make his case. And his case was essentially this: your worth is in what you do for me, not in what you become for yourself.

He didn't say it that way. He probably didn't even think of it that way. That was the story underneath the story, and my unconscious mind heard every word of it.

Here's what's wild: I almost believed him. Not because Eric was particularly convincing. But because his story and my story were running on the same frequency. *You're not smart enough for college, your worth is in serving someone else, and who do I think I am to want something bigger?* are basically the same story, wearing different clothes. They're all reading from the same script: sit down, shut up, and be grateful for your scraps.

I burned the script.

We broke up. I got accepted to Stanford. Let that sink in for a second - Stanford. I ultimately chose Santa Clara University, where I earned 50% of my tuition in scholarships and grants, spent my senior year traveling abroad, and graduated with honors in Psychology.

The girl who needed a gap year because she "wasn't smart enough" graduated with honors. $8 an hour, my ass. The filters were lying the whole time. All of that, built on the ashes of a story that almost won.

Your story is trying to win, too. The question is whether you're going to let it.

Here's Where It Gets Weird

Stay with me for a second because this is going to blow your mind.

In his groundbreaking book, "Flow: The Psychology of Optimal Experience," psychologist Mihaly Csikszentmihalyi discovered something that should make all of us stop and question everything we think we know about reality. Your brain is processing 11 million bits of information every single second.

ELEVEN. MILLION. Bits. Every. Second. Right now. While you're sitting here reading this.

Picture this: I'm standing in front of you, throwing 11 million toothpicks at you every single second. Every sight, every sound, every sensation, every smell, every taste, every signal your body is sending. Eleven million toothpicks. Per second. It's an overwhelming flood of data that would crash any computer ever built.

Now here's the part that changes everything. Your conscious mind can only catch 134 of those toothpicks.

One hundred and thirty-four. Out of eleven million.

Here's what's really happening to the rest of them. Your unconscious mind does not just ignore the toothpicks it does not pass through. It does three things. It deletes them. It distorts them. It generalizes them. All based on your filters. Your brain is not a neutral receiver of information. It is an editor. A very opinionated, heavily biased editor who has been working from the same old notes for decades.

So if your filter says money is hard, your brain deletes the opportunity, distorts the possibility, and generalizes it into "see, I knew it wouldn't work." If your filter says you are not smart enough, your brain deletes the compliment, distorts the feedback, and generalizes it into more evidence that you were right about yourself all along.

You are not seeing reality. You are seeing your filters' version of reality. And you have been mistaking it for the truth your entire life.

The real work is not adding more information to a clogged system. It is clearing out the negative thoughts, emotions, old stories we tell ourselves, and old programming that are gumming up your filters in the first place. Clean the filter, and you change what you see. Change what you see, and you change what you do. Change what you do, and you change everything.

That is not a tagline. That is the whole game.

Your brain isn't trying to sabotage you. It's trying to prove you right. Whatever story you tell it about reality, it will work overtime to collect evidence that supports that story.

This is why two people can experience the exact same event and walk away with completely different interpretations of what happened. Same 11 million bits of information, different filters, different stories, different realities.

This is why some people see opportunities everywhere while others see obstacles. Why some people bounce back from setbacks while others get stuck. Why some people create abundance while others struggle with scarcity.

It's not that they live in different worlds. They live in the same world with different stories about what that world means.

The Stories You Inherited (And How They're No Longer Serving You)

Plot twist: Most of your stories aren't even yours.

You inherited them. From your parents, your grandparents, your culture, your religion, your socioeconomic background, and every authority figure who had access to your developing brain.

Before you could walk, talk, or think critically, you were downloading stories about how the world works:

"Money doesn't grow on trees." "You have to work hard for everything you get." "Good things don't last." "People like us don't get lucky breaks." "It's selfish to want more than you need." "Rich people are greedy." "If you get too successful, people will resent you." "Don't get too big for your britches." "Stay humble." "Don't rock the boat."

Some of these stories came through direct statements. Most came through observation. You watched how your parents handled money, conflict, success, and failure. You absorbed their unconscious beliefs about what was possible for people in your family. You learned their definitions of safety, security, and appropriate ambition.

Since you were a child with a developing brain, you assumed these stories were universal truths rather than just one family's strategy for navigating their particular circumstances.

Here's the problem: The stories that helped your parents survive their world might be exactly what's limiting you in yours.

Maybe your parents grew up during economic hardship, so they developed beliefs about scarcity, saving every penny, and being grateful for what you have. Those beliefs helped them feel secure during uncertain times. If you inherited those beliefs and you're now living in abundance, those same beliefs might be preventing you from investing in new opportunities, taking calculated risks, or enjoying the wealth you've created.

Maybe your parents grew up in environments where standing out was dangerous, where tall poppies got cut down, where success made you a target, where it was safer to blend in than to shine. The beliefs they developed about humility, modesty, and not making waves helped them avoid negative attention. If you inherited those beliefs and you're now trying to build a business, make an impact, or step into leadership, those same beliefs might be sabotaging your success by limiting your visibility.

Maybe your parents experienced betrayal or abandonment, so they developed beliefs about self-reliance, emotional walls, and not trusting too easily. Those beliefs protected them from further hurt. If you inherited those beliefs, they might be preventing you from building the deep relationships and partnerships that could transform your life.

The stories that kept them safe might be keeping you small.

When Trauma Writes the Script

Sometimes our most limiting stories are born in a single moment of trauma or crisis. One event can create a story so powerful that it shapes decades of decisions.

When I was thirteen years old, my world exploded. My uncle, my mom's brother, was killed in a workplace shooting. He wasn't even supposed to be at work that day. He had gone in on his day off to drop something off in his boss's office. When an angry employee came back to shoot up the workplace, looking for that boss, who wasn't even there, my uncle was standing in the boss's office with his back to the door.

Seven people died that day. My uncle was one of them.

I remember my mom coming home inconsolable. I had never seen an adult completely fall apart like that. We packed our car and drove through the night to Oklahoma to be with family. Six months later, we moved across the country to New York.

That one event rewrote my family's entire story about safety, security, and how quickly good things can be taken away.

For my thirteen-year-old brain, trying to make sense of something senseless, that event created a story that would follow me for decades: "Good things don't last. Safety is an illusion. The people you love can be taken away in an instant. Don't get too comfortable. Don't get too attached. Don't trust that things will work out, because life can change in a heartbeat."

I didn't consciously choose this story. I was thirteen. And my unconscious mind, desperate to protect me from ever experiencing that kind of devastating loss again, created a narrative that supposedly would keep me safe: If I don't get too attached to good things, if I always keep one foot out the door, then maybe I can avoid that kind of pain again.

This story showed up everywhere. In relationships where I would sabotage things when they got too good because I was waiting for the other shoe to drop. In business where I would hold back from fully committing to opportunities because "you never know what might happen." In my inability to enjoy success because there was always this voice in the back of my head saying, "Don't get too excited. This won't last."

The story that was supposed to protect me was actually preventing me from fully experiencing love, joy, success, and connection.

Here's the thing about trauma stories: They feel so true because they're based on something that actually happened. Unlike inherited stories, which you can sometimes dismiss as "just something my parents believed," trauma stories have evidence. Something terrible did happen. People you loved were taken away. Trust was broken. Safety was shattered.

And just because something happened once doesn't mean it will happen again. Just because you experienced loss doesn't mean you're destined for more loss. Just because you were hurt doesn't mean you're fundamentally unsafe.

Trauma stories are not prophecies. They're just your brain's attempt to prevent future pain by over-preparing for danger that may never come.

The Stories That Keep You Stuck

Let me tell you about the most expensive stories people tell themselves. These are the stories that cost you money, opportunities, relationships, and years of your life:

"I'm not smart enough." This story makes you talk yourself out of opportunities before you even try. It makes you over-prepare for everything because you assume you're starting from a deficit. It makes you discount your ideas before sharing them and defer to others even when you have better solutions.

"I don't deserve good things." This story makes you sabotage success when you get it. It makes you settle for less than you want because asking for more feels greedy or inappropriate. It makes you work harder than necessary because you believe you have to earn what others get freely.

"People like me don't get lucky breaks." This story makes you blind to opportunities that are right in front of you. It makes you assume others have advantages you don't have. It makes you wait for permission instead of creating your own opportunities.

"I have to do everything myself." This story makes you reject help when it's offered. It makes you micromanage instead of delegate. It makes you burn out because you can't scale beyond your own capacity.

"Money is hard to come by." This story makes you undercharge for your services. It makes you avoid spending money on things that could make you more money. It makes you focus on saving pennies while missing opportunities to earn dollars.

"If I succeed, people will resent me." This story makes you play small to keep others comfortable. It makes you downplay your achievements and hide your ambitions. It makes you choose mediocrity to avoid standing out.

"I'm too old/young/inexperienced/damaged." This story makes you disqualify yourself before anyone else gets the chance. It makes you wait for some future version of yourself instead of working with who you are right now.

Do any of these sound familiar? They should, because these are some of the most common stories human beings tell themselves. And every single one of them is **bullshit**.

The Story That Changes Everything

Let me tell you about someone I'll call Michelle, because her story transformation will blow your mind.

When Michelle first came to work with me, she was drowning. She and her husband were $70,000 in debt, she was eight months pregnant with their second child, and she was losing sleep every night trying to figure out how they were going to survive financially with only one income.

The story Michelle was telling herself was devastating: "We're terrible with money. We always make bad decisions. We're going to be struggling forever. People like us don't get to have financial freedom; we just have to work harder and sacrifice more. This debt is proof that we're failures as adults."

This story was doing more than just making her feel bad. It was literally creating her financial reality.

When Michelle looked at their finances, all she could see were problems. The debt payments. The interest charges. The monthly expenses that seemed impossible to cover. Her brain, filtering everything through her story of financial failure, was blind to possibilities and opportunities that were sitting right in front of her.

So we changed her story.

We helped Michelle shift from "We're trapped by our financial mistakes" to "We're intelligent people who are learning to manage money strategically." From "This debt defines us as failures" to "This debt is temporary, and we have the skills to eliminate it." From "We don't have enough" to "We have more resources than we realize."

With her new story came new filters. Instead of only seeing problems, she started noticing opportunities. Instead of focusing on what they didn't have, she started looking for ways to optimize what they did have. Instead of feeling powerless, she started feeling empowered to take action.

Within 30 days - **thirty fucking days** - Michelle and her husband had paid off $50,000 of their debt.

Not because they won the lottery. Not because a rich relative died and left them money. Not because they suddenly started earning more.

They paid off $50,000 in 30 days because their new story helped them see possibilities that had been there all along. They found money in accounts they'd forgotten about. They discovered strategies for moving debt around that they hadn't considered before. They took actions that had seemed impossible when they were living in their old story.

Today, Michelle talks about having choice and abundance instead of stress and limitation.

The only thing that changed was the story and the new aligned inspired actions that came from the new story.

The Neuroscience of Story Change

Here's what's actually happening in your brain when you change a story at the unconscious level, which, not coincidentally, is exactly where the real work happens.

When you create your new story, you create new neural pathways. Your brain starts filtering for evidence that supports the new narrative instead of the old one. You begin to notice opportunities, resources, and possibilities that were always there but were invisible to you when you were living in your old story.

This isn't positive thinking or wishful thinking. This is neuroscience. Your brain's primary job is to keep you alive, and it does that by helping you navigate the world according to the stories you tell it about how the world works.

And here's the catch: Your brain doesn't like story changes. New stories feel dangerous because they're unfamiliar. Your unconscious mind would rather keep you stuck in a story that makes you miserable than risk the unknown territory of a story that could make you happy.

This is why affirmations don't work. Vision boards don't work. Deciding to "think positive" doesn't work. Not because you're doing it wrong, it's because you're working in the wrong "mind".

The story isn't living in your conscious mind. It's buried in the other one, your unconscious mind, running silently in the background, shaping every decision, every reaction, every result you're creating.

You can't think your way out of something that isn't thinking.

You have to go deeper.

Real change requires rewiring the unconscious mind. Full stop. Not as a nice idea. Not as a coaching trend. As the only place where change actually lasts. Everything else is temporary.

The Cost of Old Stories

You know that feeling when you're wearing clothes that are way too small? How everything feels constricted and uncomfortable? When you can't move freely or breathe deeply? That's what it feels like when you're living a story that no longer fits who you've become.

Maybe you've outgrown the story that you're not smart enough, and you're still talking yourself out of opportunities that require you to trust your intelligence.

Maybe you've outgrown the story that you're not worthy of love, and you're still sabotaging relationships when they get too good because deep down you're waiting for the person to figure out you're not worth it.

Maybe you've outgrown the story that you have to struggle for everything, and you're still making everything harder than it needs to be because ease feels foreign and suspicious.

Maybe you've outgrown the story that money is scarce, and you're still hoarding every penny instead of investing in opportunities that could multiply your wealth.

The problem is that these old stories feel like your identity. They feel like the truth. They feel like "just who you are." So even when they're limiting you, even when they're causing you pain, even when they're preventing you from having what you want, there's a part of you that clings to them because they're familiar and safe.

Familiar isn't the same as true. And comfortable isn't the same as beneficial.

Sometimes the story that got you here is the exact thing standing between you and where you want to be.

YOUR STORY AUDIT

Time to get brutally honest about the stories you're currently telling yourself. We're not here to judge, we're here to drag them into the light so you can decide whether they're still serving you, or whether it's time for some serious editing.

This is your cue to grab your workbook, open it to this chapter, pen in hand. The people who do the writing are the ones who get the results. The people who just read get a very interesting story to tell at dinner parties.

ROUND 1: THE MONEY STORIES

"When it comes to money, people like me always..."

"Money is..."

"Rich people are..."

"If I had more money, people would think I'm..."

ROUND 2: THE SUCCESS STORIES

"When it comes to success, I..."

"My definition of success is..."

"If I became really successful, I would lose..."

"I don't deserve success because..."

ROUND 3: THE RELATIONSHIP STORIES

"When it comes to love, I always..."

"My definition of love is..."

"If someone really knew me, they would..."

"I can't trust people because..."

ROUND 4: THE CAPABILITY STORIES

"When it comes to achieving big goals, I..."

"I'm not the kind of person who..."

"I don't have what it takes to..."

ROUND 5: THE SAFETY STORIES

"My definition of safety is..."

"The world is..."

"If I take risks, I will..."

"Good things don't last because..."

DIG DEEPER: FOR EACH STORY YOU IDENTIFIED...

Ask yourself these four questions:

1. What evidence am I constantly looking for that proves this story is true?

2. What evidence am I ignoring that contradicts this story?

3. Where did this story come from? Whose voice does it sound like?

4. If you keep living this story for the next 10 years, where will you be?

NOW WRITE YOUR NEW STORY

If you could rewrite one of the stories above, what would the new version say? Write it in your workbook. Let yourself dream a little. That conscious version, the one you just wrote, is the starting point. It's not the destination. Writing a new story plants the seed. Rewiring it at the unconscious level is what makes it grow. One is temporary. The other is permanent. And permanent is what we're after.

Remember: You are not your stories. You are the author of your stories. Every story that was written can be rewritten. Every narrative that was inherited can be updated. Every trauma-based tale can be transformed.

The question isn't whether your current stories are true. The question is whether they're useful. Are they helping you create the life you want, or are they keeping you stuck in a life you've outgrown?

Because here's what I know for sure: The story changes the filter. The filter changes what you see. What you see changes what you do. And what you do changes everything.

So stop running on old programming. You're not the same person who wrote those stories. It's time your story caught up to who you've become.

CHAPTER 3
YOUR SECRET CEO

"Until you make the unconscious conscious, it will direct your life, and you will call it fate."
— Carl Jung

Your unconscious mind is running your life, and you don't even know it.

While you've been up here making conscious decisions, setting goals, and telling yourself you're finally going to do the thing, there's been a silent CEO operating in the background. Overriding your plans. Sabotaging your progress. Keeping you locked in patterns you swore you'd break years ago.

And this CEO? It's been making decisions based on decades-old programming that your brain has literally hardwired as fact. Every trauma, every repeated experience, every emotional moment created a neural pathway, and the stronger that pathway got, the more automatic it became. Your brain wasn't broken. It was brilliant. It built the fastest, most efficient routes to keep you safe. The problem is your brain doesn't come with an expiration system. Those pathways don't dissolve just because the danger has passed. They keep firing. The survival strategy that protected you at five is still running at thirty-five, just in a completely different life, against completely different circumstances, causing completely different damage. That's not protection anymore.

That's a prison.

This CEO isn't malicious. It's not trying to ruin your life. It's just working from a very old playbook. And that playbook? It's running approximately 95% of your daily decisions.

Ninety. Five. Percent.

Your conscious mind, the part that made your vision board, set your intentions, and signed up for every personal development program you've ever bought, is running about 5% of the show. It's not the CEO. It's not even the VP. It's the well-meaning intern who keeps submitting ideas that the CEO quietly ignores.

I know. It's a lot.

Here's why this is actually the best news you've ever heard: once you understand how this CEO operates, you can stop fighting yourself and start working with the most powerful part of your mind instead of against it.

You just have to meet it first.

The Mind You Don't Know You Have

Let's start with some mind-blowing facts that no one ever taught you about your own brain.

Neuroscientist Dr. David Eagleman puts it bluntly: "your conscious mind is like a tiny rowboat on top of a massive ocean of unconscious processing. The ocean is moving whether the rowboat knows it or not." Research suggests the unconscious mind processes information up to 500,000 times faster than conscious thought, which means by the time you think you made a decision, the real decision was already made. Your conscious mind just got the memo late.

Your unconscious mind controls 95% of your daily activities. Every breath. Every heartbeat. The love you feel for your kids that hits before a single thought forms. The way certain music moves you to tears before you even know why. The way your whole body relaxes around people who feel safe. How you fall in love before your conscious mind has even run a background check. The way a smell can teleport you back twenty years in an instant. The excitement that takes over your whole body when you're on the right path. The gut feeling that something is wrong before anything has happened. The tension in your shoulders when your phone rings and it's *that* person. The way you shrink in certain rooms without deciding to. The patterns that keep tripping you up, no matter how many times you swear you're done with them. The reactions that come out before you even choose them.

Your unconscious mind doesn't judge what it runs. It just runs it. The magic and the mess. All day. Every day. Without asking your permission.

Your unconscious mind stores every single experience you've ever had. Every conversation, every emotion, every sensory detail from your entire life is filed away in there. All 11 million bits of information per second, aka toothpicks. Most of it you can't consciously access, and it's all influencing your behavior.

Your unconscious mind doesn't understand time. To your unconscious mind, that traumatic experience from when you were seven years old is happening right now. That limiting decision you made when you were twelve is still active today. That fear you developed when you were fifteen is still driving your choices.

Your unconscious mind takes everything literally. It doesn't understand negatives, sarcasm, metaphors, or "just kidding." If you constantly say "I'm so stupid" when you make mistakes, your unconscious mind files that under "facts about me" and starts creating evidence to prove it.

Your unconscious mind's primary job is to keep you alive, not to make you happy (I know, that sucks, right?). It will choose familiar misery over unfamiliar joy every single time because familiar feels safe, even when familiar is slowly killing you.

Still think you're in control of your decisions? Think again.

Let me tell you about a client I'll call David, who learned this the hard way. David came to me because he couldn't figure out why he kept sabotaging every business opportunity that came his way. Consciously, he wanted success. He had great ideas, solid strategies, and all the skills he needed.

And every time he got close to a breakthrough, something would happen. He'd pick a fight with a potential business partner. He'd miss an important deadline. He'd suddenly decide the opportunity "wasn't right for him" and walk away.

David was convinced he was just unlucky or that success wasn't meant for him. What he didn't realize was that his unconscious mind was running a program installed when he was eight years old.

When David was eight, his dad started a business that failed spectacularly. David watched his family lose their house, his parents fight constantly about money, and his dad sink into depression. His eight-year-old brain made a decision: "A successful business leads to family destruction."

For thirty years, that unconscious program had been protecting David from the "danger" of a successful business by sabotaging him every time he got close. His unconscious mind would rather keep him safely unsuccessful than risk the family destruction it believed success would bring.

Once we identified and cleared that program, David's entire business trajectory changed. Within six months, he had launched the most successful venture of his career.

My Own Unconscious Wake-Up Call

I lived this reality firsthand when I was struggling with infertility for three and a half years. My husband (now ex-husband) and I were doing everything "right", seeing specialists, following protocols, timing everything perfectly. And nothing was working.

Consciously, I wanted a baby more than anything. I was doing everything the doctors told me to do.

What I didn't understand then was that my unconscious mind was working against me.

I was stressed out of my mind. I was working as an executive assistant to the CEO of a multi-billion-dollar company, taking calls at 3 AM to talk to suppliers in China, working on Sundays, and living in constant high-alert mode. My doctor kept telling me that stress was likely a major factor, but I couldn't see how to change it.

What I realize now is that my unconscious mind had programs running that were directly sabotaging my fertility:

"You have to work harder than everyone else to be worthy" (instilled from childhood messages about being "too much"). "Success requires sacrifice" (learned from watching my dad work 40+ years at IBM). "You can't have everything you want" (generalized from various childhood disappointments).

My body was literally rejecting pregnancy because my unconscious mind believed I couldn't handle both career success and motherhood. The stress wasn't just external; it was being generated by unconscious programs that were convinced I had to choose.

The moment I quit that corporate job and went full-time into my wedding consulting business, following my entrepreneurial instincts instead of the "safe" corporate path, and rewiring those unconscious patterns, I got pregnant within months with my first. Then with my second, I got pregnant when I planned to, no waiting, no more years of trying with no results, it was easy and effortless.

The Filter System That Controls Your Reality

Remember those 11 million toothpicks from Chapter 2, and the 134 your conscious mind actually catches? Let's go deeper into how your unconscious mind decides which 134 toothpicks you get to consciously experience.

Your unconscious mind runs everything through a sophisticated filter system made up of:

Your Memories: Every experience you've ever had creates a reference point for how to interpret new experiences. If you got rejected when you tried to speak up in third grade, your unconscious mind might filter all future speaking opportunities through that lens of potential humiliation or rejection.

Your Beliefs: These are the "rules" your unconscious mind thinks are true about how the world works. "People can't be trusted." "Money is the root of all evil." "I have to work hard to be worthy of love." These beliefs act like invisible rules that determine what you notice and what you ignore.

Your Values: These are what your unconscious mind has decided are most important. And here's the kicker: your unconscious values might be completely different from what you think your conscious values are. You might consciously value adventure while unconsciously valuing security, which is why you keep talking yourself out of taking risks.

Your Language Patterns: The words you use literally shape your reality. If you speak "victim language" ("This always happens to me," "I never get lucky," "Life is hard"), your unconscious mind creates a victim reality. If you speak "ownership language" ("How can I solve this?" "What's the opportunity here?" "What can I learn from this?"), You get an ownership reality.

Your Decisions: Not just the big conscious decisions, the thousands of micro-decisions you make every day about what things mean, how to respond, and what's possible. Most of these decisions happen so fast you don't even realize you're making them.

Your Life Experiences: Everything that has happened to you becomes a data point for how to navigate similar situations in the future. The problem is, your unconscious mind is really bad at recognizing when situations are actually different from past experiences.

And those are just the filters we can name in a single chapter. We can go several layers deeper (not here, though, we'd be here for another 100 pages if we did) because the truth is your filter system is far more complex and far more personal than any list can capture. Most people never even know these deeper filters exist. They just wonder why they keep hitting the same invisible walls, no matter how hard they try. That is not a willpower problem. That is a filter problem.

These filters work together to create your personal reality bubble. And the scary part is you think your reality bubble is reality. You think everyone sees the world the same way you do. You think your interpretation of events is the objective truth.

It's not. It's just your unconscious mind's best guess, based on outdated programming. The filter doesn't lie to you on purpose — it just runs the program you gave it. Shift the program, and the entire experience of the world shifts with it.

The Four Voices That Run Your Life

Inside your unconscious mind, there are four distinct voices that are constantly influencing your decisions. Most people have no idea these voices exist, which is why they keep getting blindsided by their own behavior.

Three of these voices are lying to you, causing negative inner dialogue that's sabotaging your success. One of them never has. The problem is that most people have the volume settings completely backwards. That fourth voice is your intuition. The one that sees you the way Source sees you. The one that never bought the story, never joined the chorus of doubt, and never for a single second stopped having your back. Everything else is noise. This one is the truth.

Voice #1: The Inner Ego

The inner ego is the protector of your identity. Not your true identity. The identity you built when something happened that you were not equipped to handle. When a need went unmet. When you were hurt, dismissed, overlooked, or told you were not enough in some way. Your inner ego stepped in, built a story around that wound, and has been defending that story ever since.

This is the voice of the labels you gave yourself and the identity you constructed around those labels. Smart or not smart enough. Strong or not strong enough. Worthy or completely undeserving. You adopted these labels from your environment, your experiences, your family, and a world that was constantly telling you who you were before you were old enough to decide for yourself, and these created your filters.

And now your inner ego will go to war to protect them.

It shows up as defiance. Stubbornness. Rigidity. An absolute refusal to see things differently, admit to being wrong, or consider that another way might exist. Not because you are a difficult person. It simply is because your inner ego genuinely believes that if you let go of that identity, even the painful parts of it, something worse will happen. Exposure. Vulnerability. The thing it has been protecting you from all along.

Here is what is important to understand. Like all the voices, the inner ego was never trying to hurt you. It was trying to keep you safe. It just digs in harder than the others. It mistakes rigidity for strength and confuses stubbornness with survival. And the longer it has been protecting a particular wound, the harder it fights when anyone or anything gets close to it.

The inner ego does not need to be destroyed. It needs to be understood. Because the moment you understand what it is protecting and why, you can finally permit it to stand down.

The Inner Ego sounds like:

- "I don't need help. I've got this."
- "I'm not wrong. They just don't understand me."
- "I've always done it this way, and it works fine."
- "If I admit I was wrong, it means I'm weak."
- "I can't let them see me struggle. That's not who I am."
- "Why would I change? This is just how I am."
- "I don't need to hear this. I already know."
- "If I let go of this, who am I even supposed to be?"

The inner ego is not trying to keep you stuck. It is trying to keep you safe. The problem is that it cannot tell the difference between the two. Familiar feels safe even when familiar is in a cage. And your inner ego will choose that cage every single time over the terrifying, exhilarating, necessary work of becoming someone new.

Which brings us to the voice that makes sure you never forget why you shouldn't even try.

Voice #2: The Inner Critic

You know that voice that shows up the second you think about doing something bigger, something bolder, something that actually matters to you? The one that immediately rattles off every reason why you should not, cannot, and will not? That is your inner critic. And when people say you are your own worst enemy, this is exactly who they are talking about.

The inner critic is the voice of judgment. Not judgment from the outside world, it's the far more brutal kind you dish out to yourself. It does not believe life can be better than it is right now. It cannot see past the current moment into what is possible. Even if your life right now is genuinely painful, even if you are miserable, even if you know something has to change, your inner critic will fight hard to keep things exactly as they are. Because to the inner critic, the devil you know will always be safer than the devil you don't.

It is not trying to destroy you. It genuinely believes it is keeping you safe by cataloguing every reason why trying is dangerous, why failing is inevitable, and why staying put is the only logical choice. Its entire protection strategy is to keep you small, keep you stuck, and make sure you never rattle the bars of the cage it has spent years carefully building around you.

The Inner Critic sounds like:

- "You're not good enough for that."
- "Who do you think you are?"
- "You're going to embarrass yourself."
- "Remember what happened last time you tried something like this?"
- "People like you don't get to have nice things."
- "You're too old, too young, too inexperienced, too far behind."
- "Everyone is going to find out you have no idea what you are doing."
- "Don't even try. You already know how this ends."

The inner critic is not your truth. It is your fear wearing a very convincing disguise. And the longer you have been listening to it, the more real it sounds. Here is what it won't do. It won't throw a tantrum to get what it wants. That job belongs to a very different voice.

Voice #3: The Inner Child

You know the person in the meeting who takes every piece of feedback as a personal attack? The one who shuts down when things do not go their way, disappears when conflict arises, or explodes over something that seems completely disproportionate to the situation? That is not an adult having a bad day. That is an inner child who never got what it needed and never forgot it.

Your inner child is where hurt lives. Where betrayal lives. Where every unmet need, every moment you were not seen, not chosen, not protected, not loved the way you needed to be loved got filed away and stored. It carries every wound from before puberty, the good stuff and the painful stuff, and it has been quietly running reactions in your adult life ever since.

When your inner child is the one driving, it does not respond to situations the way they actually are. It responds to how they feel compared to something that happened a long time ago. Someone cancels plans, and suddenly it is not just a scheduling conflict; it is abandonment. Someone gives you constructive feedback, and it is not just an opinion; it is proof that you are not enough. Someone raises their voice, and it is not just a heated conversation; it is every time you were small and scared and had no control over what happened next.

The inner child's response to all of this is to do what it learned to do back then. Hide. Avoid. Shrink. Make yourself as small and invisible as possible so nothing else can hurt you.

And when the inner child cannot hide anymore, the inner ego shows up to finish the job. They work together like a security system: the inner child feels the threat, and the inner ego slams the door. The stubbornness you see in the inner ego is often not really about the surface identity it's protecting. It's about the wounded child behind that identity that it refuses to let anyone see.

The Inner Child sounds like:

- "That's not fair."
- "Nobody understands me."
- "Why does this always happen to me?"
- "I just want to be seen."
- "If I disappear, maybe it won't hurt as much."
- "I knew they would leave eventually."
- "I don't feel safe enough to try."
- "I just need someone to tell me it is going to be okay."
- "Why do I always end up here?"

Your inner child is not broken. It is not weak. It is a part of you that got hurt before it had any tools to process that hurt, and has been doing its best ever since, with what it had. And here is what it cannot do on its own. It cannot see that you are not that child anymore. It cannot see that you have choices now that you did not have then. It cannot see that the thing it is hiding from is not actually as dangerous as it remembers. It is frozen in the moment the wound happened, waiting for someone to come back and make it right.

That someone is you. And that work begins when you finally stop letting your inner child make adult decisions.

Voice #4: Your Intuition (The One True Voice)

Now we get to the one that matters most.

While the inner critic was busy telling you why you cannot, the inner child was hiding from what might hurt, and the inner ego was slamming doors to protect what was wounded underneath, your intuition has been quietly in the background this entire time. Waiting. Whispering. Sending signals you wrote off as coincidence, nervousness, or wishful thinking.

It was none of those things. It was you. Your highest you. Trying to get through.

The Oxford Dictionary of Psychology defines intuition as "immediate understanding, knowing or awareness, derived neither from perception nor from reasoning." In other words, it is not something you think your way into. It is something you already know before your brain has had a chance to argue with it. It is your gut feelings, your simple knowing, your inner wisdom that exists completely independent of logic, evidence, or anyone else's opinion.

Your intuition is the translator between your conscious and unconscious mind. It is the channel through which your higher self communicates what your filters, your wounds, and your bullshit cannot. It does not operate from fear. It does not deal in shame, judgment, or worst-case scenarios. It simply knows. And it has always known. You just could not always hear it over the volume of the other three.

Here is what makes your intuition completely different from every other voice in your head. **It is ALWAYS kind. Not always gentle**! Sometimes it will tap you on the shoulder softly. Sometimes it will send you a gut punch so undeniable you have to sit down. Sometimes it will give you an A-Ha so big it rearranges everything you thought you knew.

We have a name for those gut-punch A-Ha moments. We call it getting a "Wanda." Named after "A Fish Called Wanda" because sometimes your intuition does not tap you gently on the shoulder like a polite houseguest. Sometimes it hauls off and smacks you in the face with a dead fish. Lovingly. With your best interests at heart. And still very much a dead fish to the face. Our clients wear their "Wandas" like a badge of honor. If you got a big Wanda, something real just happened.

And if the voice in your head is negative, critical, fearful, or unkind? That is not your intuition. Full stop. Your intuition does not tear you down. It does not catastrophize. It does not whisper that you are not enough. Those voices have names, and we already covered them. Your intuition only ever points toward your highest good, your next level, and the version of you that you came here to become.

Think of it like a GPS. It does not judge you for taking a wrong turn. It does not sigh heavily and remind you of all the other wrong turns you have taken. It simply recalibrates and says here is your new route. You cannot make a wrong choice when you are following your intuition. Every path is either the direction you were meant to take or a lesson you were meant to have. Either way, it is moving you forward. Either way, it is serving you.

Your intuition sounds like:

- "This feels right."
- "Trust the process."
- "You've got this."
- "Follow this path."
- "Everything is working out for you."
- "This is the one."
- "Let go. It is safe."
- "You already know the answer."

One last thing about your intuition that nobody tells you about. Learning to work with it is a four-part journey, and most people never make it past the first step.

First, you have to understand that you have one. This sounds obvious, but for people who have spent decades drowning in the noise of the other three voices, it is anything but. Your intuition has been there your entire life. It never left. It never gave up on you. You just stopped being able to hear it.

Second, you have to learn how it communicates with you specifically. Because your intuition does not speak the same language to everyone. Some people see it: a flash of imagery, a vision, a knowing that arrives visually. Some people feel it: a physical sensation, a gut punch, a warmth, or a tightening in the body that tells them everything they need to know. Some people hear it: a quiet voice, a word, a phrase that drops in from nowhere and lands like truth. And some people simply know it: no explanation, no evidence, just an unshakeable certainty that arrives fully formed. Your job is to learn your own language.

Third, and this is the hardest part… you have to learn to trust it. Because your intuition will ask you to do things that do not always make logical sense. It will point you toward doors that look closed. It will redirect you away from things that look perfect on paper. It will ask you to leap before you can see the landing. And every single one of the other three voices will have opinions about that. Loud ones. Learning to trust your intuition over the noise of the inner critic, the inner child, and the inner ego is the most courageous work you will ever do.

Fourth, and most important, you have to take inspired action in the physical world. Because intuition without action is just a feeling. The magic happens when you hear it, trust it, and then actually move. When you let it lead you somewhere, your logical mind never would have gone on its own.

Your intuition is a knowing that allows you to live as your true, authentic self. It has your best interest at heart. It does not judge, criticize, or create fear. It simply guides. Always forward. Always toward what is best for you. Always toward who you were always meant to be.

Your intuition has never lied to you. It has never stopped having your back. It has never once seen you as anything less than the fullest, most extraordinary version of yourself. It is how Source sees you. It always has been.

It's time to turn up the volume.

The Cost of Unconscious Living

Most people live their entire lives being unconsciously controlled by programming they did not choose and do not even know exists. They wonder why they keep getting the same results, attracting the same types of people, and facing the same challenges over and over again. Same relationship dynamic, different person. Same money ceiling, different business. Same self-sabotage, different situation. Just enough variation in the packaging to make it look like a new problem when it is actually the same old program running on repeat.

They think they need more willpower. A better morning routine. The right mentor. The perfect strategy. One more course, one more certification. And honestly, they are half right. The course and certification part...that is actually the answer. Just not the ones that pile more conscious information onto an unconscious problem. The ones that go in and do the actual rewiring. That is the difference between collecting knowledge and creating transformation.

Here's the truth: Willpower is a conscious tool trying to override an unconscious force. And the unconscious wins that battle every single time. It is not even a fair fight. Sending willpower to fix unconscious programming is like showing up to a gunfight with a strongly worded letter. Brave. Adorable. Completely ineffective.

The strategies are not the problem. The circumstances are not the problem. The market, the economy, the timing, the algorithm, not Mercury being in fucking retrograde. None of it is the problem. The programming is the problem. And the programming lives somewhere that vision boards, positive thinking, and sheer determination simply cannot reach.

Here is what I know after working with thousands of people across every industry, income level, and life circumstance: the ones who transform are not the ones who try harder. They are not the ones who want it more or hustle longer or wake up at 5 am and cold plunge their way to enlightenment. The ones who transform are the ones who finally stop trying to outrun their programming and decide to actually change it instead.

That decision changes everything.

The Battle for Your Mind

Here's what's happening in your head every single day: Your inner ego, inner critic, and inner child are the voices of your resistance. They create stress, overwhelm, exhaustion, and make everything feel harder than it needs to be. They're the reason you lack inspiration, second-guess yourself, and feel stuck.

Your intuition, on the other hand, is the voice that solves the challenges created by your resistance. It's the voice that helps you manifest what you truly want with ease and flow.

When the first three voices are running the show, you feel it: life is hard, nothing flows, you're stressed, exhausted, and wondering why everything requires so much effort. When your intuition is running the show, you feel that too: things click, solutions appear, you're inspired and moving with instead of against yourself. The goal isn't to silence your inner ego, inner critic, and inner child; they have their uses. The goal is to turn their volume down and your intuition's volume way up.

Because here's the truth: Your inner ego, inner critic, and inner child are loud. They scream. They demand attention. They create drama, urgency, and crisis. They run around like a bull in a china shop and come out without you asking for them.

Your intuition is quiet. It whispers. It suggests rather than demands. It trusts rather than forces. It will always come when asked, and it has to be asked.

And in a world that rewards the loudest voice, most people miss the wisest one.

I watched this play out firsthand with my former business partner, Sarah. Four voices, four agendas, one decision, and she fed the wrong three. The full cost of that is a story for later. Right now, what matters is this:

One decision. Four voices. Everything depends on which ones you feed.

How My Unconscious Mind Nearly Destroyed Everything

I have run a lot of programs in my life. The most costly one was not a course, not a launch, not a bad business decision. It was an unconscious belief I did not even know I was carrying.

For years, I had this unconscious program running that said, "Entrepreneurs are shysters who flash money and can't be trusted." This came directly from my family's reaction to my grandfather, who was a successful real estate agent. Instead of celebrating his success, family members would whisper things like "He's just a shyster" or "He's always flashing his money around."

My five-year-old brain absorbed this message: "Entrepreneurship = being a bad and untrustworthy person."

So even as I was building successful businesses, wedding consulting, network marketing, and coaching, I was unconsciously sabotaging myself because I didn't want to be seen as a "shyster."

This showed up as:

- Severely undercharging for my services
- Downplaying my success
- Feeling guilty when I made good money
- Choosing the "safe" corporate path over entrepreneurial ventures
- Always having a backup plan because "entrepreneurship isn't reliable."

The irony is not lost on me. While I was unconsciously capping my own success to avoid becoming someone I did not want to be, I was actually doing the very thing I feared most: failing the people I was meant to serve. Undercharging. Playing small. Showing up as a fraction of what I was actually capable of because some decades-old program had decided that fully stepping into my power made me the villain of someone else's story.

The moment I cleared it and installed a new belief: successful entrepreneurs serve the world by fully owning their gifts… something shifted. Not gradually. Not slowly. The kind of shift that makes you wonder what took you so long and grieve a little for the years you spent playing smaller than you were.

Within six months, I had tripled my prices. I was attracting clients who valued the work the way it deserved to be valued. My income increased by 400%. Not because I suddenly became more skilled. Not because I worked harder or hustled differently. It was because I finally stopped unconsciously dismantling my own success before it could reach me.

Your Unconscious Programs Are Running the Show

Here's a fun fact! The majority of your unconscious programming was installed before you were seven years old.

Think about it like this. The strategies your brain developed when you were a kindergartener are still running your adult life.

When you were little, your brain was like a sponge, absorbing everything around you and making meaning out of it. And here's the problem: little kids are terrible at making accurate meaning out of complex situations.

If your parents fought about money, your five-year-old brain might have decided "Money causes pain." If a teacher criticized you for being too loud, your six-year-old brain might have concluded: "It's not safe to take up space." If your dad was emotionally unavailable, your seven-year-old brain might have determined, "I'm not worth paying attention to."

These childhood conclusions became unconscious programs that are still running your life today. You might consciously know that money doesn't cause pain, and if your unconscious mind is still running the "money causes pain" program, you'll unconsciously sabotage every opportunity to create wealth.

You might consciously know that you deserve love, and if your unconscious mind is still running the "I'm not worth paying attention to" program, you'll unconsciously choose emotionally unavailable partners.

You might consciously know that you're capable and intelligent, and if your unconscious mind is still running the "it's not safe to take up space" program, you'll unconsciously shrink in situations where you could shine.

The Programming Installation Process

Let me tell you exactly how these unconscious programs get installed, because understanding this process is the first step to changing it.

Step 1: The Significant Emotional Event. Something happens that creates a strong emotional reaction. This could be trauma, but it doesn't have to be. It could be something as simple as getting laughed at when you tried to sing, being ignored when you had something important to say, or watching your parents stress about money.

Step 2: The Limiting Decision. Your brain immediately tries to make sense of what happened by asking, "What does this mean about me and how I fit in the world?" The meaning your brain creates becomes a limiting decision.

Step 3: The Generalization. Your brain takes this one experience and generalizes it to all similar situations. If you get rejected by one person, your brain might generalize that to "People will reject me if they really know me."

Step 4: The Program Installation. This limiting decision becomes an unconscious program that runs automatically in all similar situations. You don't consciously choose to run this program; it just runs in the background like malware on your computer.

Step 5: The Evidence Collection. Your unconscious mind starts filtering for evidence that proves this program is true. It notices every piece of evidence that supports the limiting decision and ignores evidence that contradicts it.

Step 6: The Self-Fulfilling Prophecy The program influences your behavior in ways that actually create the very outcomes you're trying to avoid. If you believe people will reject you, you might act defensively or withdraw, which actually pushes people away.

This is how a single childhood experience can create decades of limitation.

Let me show you how this plays out in real life. I had a client I'll call Charlie. He came to me frustrated and exhausted. He'd been "working on his business" for five years and had almost nothing to show for it. He thought he needed better strategies, more discipline, or maybe he just wasn't cut out for entrepreneurship.

What Charlie actually needed was to clear the unconscious programs that were sabotaging every strategy he tried.

Every time his business started gaining momentum, Charlie would make a decision that killed his progress, an old program protecting him from success, because it believed successful people become arrogant and lose their friends. He said yes to every request that came his way, even when it meant neglecting his own priorities, because disappointing people felt more dangerous than disappointing himself. He spent months perfecting products that never launched because they were never "ready", using impossible standards to avoid criticism that would prove he wasn't enough. And he hoarded money instead of investing in growth, because an old program said spending money meant ending up broke like his parents.

Four unconscious programs. Each one a protection strategy. Each one was destroying his chances of creating the life he wanted.

Once we cleared these programs and installed new ones aligned with his goals, Charlie's business transformed. Within eight months, he had launched three successful programs, built a community full of support, and hit his first six-figure year.

Charlie did not need a better strategy. He needed someone to help him see the programming that was quietly running his strategy into the ground. Because here is the truth: you cannot see your own blind spots. That is literally what makes them blind spots. Eight months of the right work with the right support beats years of white-knuckling his way through business and wondering why nothing was sticking.

The Unconscious Values That Really Run Your Life

Here's something that will probably piss you off: Your unconscious values are probably completely different from what you think your values are.

You might think you value success, but unconsciously value predictability. So every time you get close to a breakthrough, your unconscious mind slams the brakes. Not because you do not want it. Because wanting it and having it are two completely different levels of scary.

You might think you value freedom, but you unconsciously value safety and security above everything else. So you play it safe, stay in your lane, and keep everyone around you comfortable. Then ten years go by, and you cannot figure out why you feel like you are suffocating inside a life that looks perfectly fine on paper.

You might think you value abundance but unconsciously believe that ease is a trap. So you over-complicate the simple things. You overwork the things that are already working. You feel vaguely guilty on the good days and strangely comfortable on the hard ones. Not because you love suffering. Because somewhere in your programming is a very old invoice that keeps telling you the bill is not settled yet.

Your unconscious values were formed early in life based on what you needed to survive your particular childhood circumstances. If love was conditional in your family, you might have unconsciously decided that approval is more important than authenticity. If resources were scarce, you might have unconsciously decided that security is more important than growth.

These unconscious values act like invisible rules that govern your decisions. And until you become conscious of them, they'll continue to run your life.

Here is a pattern worth examining in your own business. Ask yourself honestly, are you attracting clients who value you or clients who need you?

Because those are two completely different unconscious programs producing two completely different results. The need to be needed is a common conflicting value we've uncovered. It looks like integrity and service on the surface. Underneath it is an old childhood program that learned love and attention came from being helpful and solving other people's problems. And it will quietly run your pricing, your client selection, and your energy levels into the ground until you shine a light on it and decide to invest in yourself to change it.

Awareness is Freedom

Your unconscious mind has been running the show for decades. It has been making decisions, filtering reality, protecting old wounds, and keeping you looping through the same patterns like a Netflix series that got renewed one too many seasons. And it has been doing all of this completely without your awareness or your permission.

Awareness is the beginning of freedom. The moment you can see the program, you are no longer completely at its mercy. You can name the voice. You can trace the pattern. You can finally understand why you keep doing what you do, even when you absolutely know better. And with the right tools and the right support, you can change it. Not manage it. Not white knuckle your way around it. Not build an elaborate system of habits and hacks to keep it temporarily at bay. Actually, change it. At the level where it lives. Permanently.

You did not survive everything you have survived, do everything you have done, and read all the way to the end of this very long chapter just to close the book, say "wow, that was interesting," and go back to doing the exact same thing you were doing before. The programming had its run. It served its purpose. It is done now. You came here to unlock what was always yours.

YOUR UNCONSCIOUS MIND AUDIT

You just spent an entire chapter meeting the voices that have been running your life, learning how your filters have been shaping your reality, and discovering that 95% of everything you think, feel, and decide has been happening without your conscious permission. That is a lot. Take a breath. Now go get your workbook, because what comes next is where the real work lives, and your inner critic is already trying to convince you that just reading this chapter counts. It does not. Pen out. Let's go.

THE VOICE AUDIT

For the next 24 hours, become a detective of your own mind. You are not here to judge what you find. You are not here to fix anything yet. You are simply here to collect data. Every time you catch yourself doing any of the following, write it down in your workbook:

- Hesitating before sending a message you already know is right.
- Shrinking in a conversation where you had something important to say.
- Saying yes when every part of you wanted to say no.
- Talking yourself out of an opportunity before you even fully explore it.
- Reacting to something in a way that felt disproportionate to what actually happened.
- Feeling guilty for something that does not actually deserve guilt.
- Avoiding a decision you already know the answer to.

For each moment, write down what happened, which voice you think was responsible, and if you can, notice what your intuition was quietly trying to say underneath all the noise.

At the end of 24 hours, look at your list. Count how many times each voice showed up. Most people are genuinely shocked by what they find. Not because the voices are new, just because they have never stopped long enough to actually see them in action. Awareness is the beginning of freedom. This exercise makes the invisible visible. And once you can see it, you can never fully unsee it.

THE MOVIE THEATER

This exercise is not something you do with a pen. It is something you do with your eyes closed and your defenses down.

We have created a guided meditation specifically for your 4 voices that will walk you through the entire experience. In it, you will meet all four voices, watch them interact, check their volume, and finally hear what your intuition has been trying to say underneath all the noise.

Scan the QR code below to access it before you continue.

Find somewhere quiet. Put your phone on do not disturb. Give yourself a space where nobody needs anything from you. Then press play and let it take you where you need to go.

When you are done, come back to this page in your workbook and journal freely about what came up. What did you see? What surprised you? What did your intuition say that the other voices have been drowning out? What do you now know that you cannot unknow?

THE FIVE-YEAR LETTER

Here is what you are going to do. You are going to write a letter. And it's not from where you are now. From five years in the future. From the version of you who finally stopped letting the inner critic run the commentary, finally stopped letting the inner child make the big decisions, finally stopped letting the inner ego defend the identity that was never really yours in the first place, and started following the one voice that never once lied to you.

That version of you exists. They are not a fantasy. They are not wishful thinking. They are the you that your intuition has been pointing toward this entire time. And they have things they desperately need you to hear right now.

Write that version's letter. Let it be long. Let it get emotional. Let it get specific. Let yourself write things that feel uncomfortably true. That discomfort is not a warning. It is your intuition finally getting loud enough to be heard.

Start with: *"I want you to know that everything you are afraid of right now..."*

Now, once you've finished the letter, answer these from your future self's perspective:

- What did you finally say yes to that changed everything?
- What did you stop tolerating the moment you started trusting yourself?
- What do you wish your past self had stopped being so afraid of?
- What became possible the moment you stopped letting the wrong voices run the show?
- What do you need your past self to know right now more than anything else?

Now read that letter back to yourself out loud. Every word of it. Because that is not fiction. That is your intuition. That is how Source has always seen you. And that version of you is not five years away. They are one decision away.

The Good News About Your Unconscious Mind

Your unconscious mind isn't your enemy. It's just been working with outdated software.

Your unconscious mind is incredibly powerful. It can process massive amounts of information, make complex connections, solve problems while you sleep, and create miraculous changes in your life.

The same unconscious mind that's been limiting you can become your greatest ally in creating the life you want. First, you have to understand how to communicate with it, how to update its programming, and how to align it with your conscious desires.

Your unconscious mind is like having a supercomputer that's been running Windows 95 for the last thirty years. It's not that the computer is broken; it just needs an operating system upgrade.

You are not your unconscious programming. You are the awareness that can observe your unconscious programming. And anything that can be observed can be changed.

Because your unconscious mind is waiting for new instructions. It's been running the same old programs for decades, and it's ready for an upgrade.

CHAPTER 4
STOP BEING THE VICTIM OF YOUR OWN LIFE

"Between stimulus and response, there is space. In that space is our power to choose our response. In our response lies our growth and our freedom."
— Viktor E. Frankl

Here is something I need to tell you right now, before we go any further: You are not a victim of your life. You are, however, possibly a victim of your own bullshit. And yes, I mean that with complete love.

Before you throw this book across the room and compose a strongly worded mental letter to me, I see you. I hear you. Real, terrible, unfair things have happened to you. Things you did not ask for, did not deserve, and would never wish on anyone. That is real, and it matters, and we are not glossing over any of it with a highlighter and a good attitude.

And here is the part that is actually the most exciting news in this entire book: the way you've been responding to those things? That's on you. And that means you have way more power in this situation than you've been giving yourself credit for. Like, a LOT more.

Two Places. One Choice. Every Single Time.

In every moment of your life, you are operating from one of two places. Cause or Effect. There is no third option. No neutral. No Switzerland of personal responsibility. Just these two, and whichever one you are living in right now is building your life, whether you realize it or not.

Effect is where most people live. Here's the thing about Effect. It is sneaky as hell. It does not show up wearing a sign that says "hello, I am your victim mentality." It shows up dressed as logic. As realism. Just telling the truth about what happened. It sounds completely reasonable from the inside. That is what makes it so dangerous.

It is focused on reasons and excuses. Blaming, shaming, and justifying. Making assumptions and judgments that turn into a completely skewed interpretation of everything that happens. Shutting down new perspectives. Getting defensive. Running on fear, anger, sadness, hurt, guilt, and shame like they are a personality. Bouncing between hiding from everything on one end and picking fights on the other. Seeing yourself as a victim of circumstance, which means in your world, everyone and everything is either against you or indifferent to you. Things are happening TO you, and you cannot see your own fingerprints on any of it.

This is the part nobody puts in the brochure. Being in Effect long enough stops being just a mindset. It goes physiological. Cortisol and adrenaline flood your system. Your vision literally narrows. Not metaphorically. Literally. You can only see one or two possibilities where dozens actually exist. Long term Effect is the precursor to dis-ease. It is why you are exhausted. It is why you feel like you are pushing through wet cement every single day. Your nervous system is running a full threat response to a life that is not actually trying to kill you. It is just not cooperating with you right now. Big difference.

Cause is a completely different experience in your body. Dopamine and serotonin show up at the party. Your eyes dilate and open up. Suddenly, you see choices and opportunities and solutions that were genuinely invisible to you thirty seconds ago from Effect. You take responsibility for your thoughts, emotions, and behaviors, not because you are a masochist but because you understand that responsibility is where your power lives. You get curious instead of defensive. Creative instead of reactionary. Proactive instead of just surviving until Friday.

Cause also changes the way you talk. Not in a fake positive-affirmations-in-the-mirror kind of way. In a completely different linguistic structure kind of way. At Cause your language is full of ownership. "I have not found the right positioning yet." "I have not communicated my expectations clearly enough." "I am calling in clients who match where I was, not where I am going." Notice how in every single one of those sentences, you are the subject. The one with the pen. The one writing the next line. Your words stop being a description of what is happening around you and start being a declaration of what you are choosing to do about it. One small shift in how you speak. An entirely different universe of available action.

Being at cause feels better. Not in a bypassing-reality, pretending-everything-is-fine kind of way. Actually better. In your body. You are not carrying the weight of a story about why things are the way they are. You are just moving. Deciding. Adjusting. Going. There is a lightness to it that most people have not felt in so long that they have forgotten it is available to them. When you are at Cause, the energy that comes back into your body is almost disorienting at first. Like taking off a backpack you forgot you were wearing.

Taking ownership of your results is not the same as taking blame for everything that has ever happened to you. Cause means that regardless of what happened, regardless of who did what and whether they deserved any of it, you are the one who gets to decide who you become on the other side of it. That is actually an enormous amount of power when you sit with it. You are not at the mercy of your history. You are not defined by the thing that hurt you, or the year that broke you, or the person who let you down. You get to decide. You get to choose. You get to write what comes next. Ownership is not a burden. It is the most liberating thing you will ever pick up.

When you live predominantly at Cause: not perfectly, not every single minute, just predominantly, your results start shifting in ways that feel almost unreasonable. You start having conversations you have been avoiding for months and discovering they go better than the three-week anxiety spiral you put yourself through anticipating them. You start making decisions faster because you are moving from intention and adjusting as you go. You start attracting clients, opportunities, and relationships that match the version of you who shows up at Cause, because that is the version of you that is finally fully visible. You stop shrinking. You stop waiting. You stop hedging. Cause makes you magnetic. Not because you became someone different. Because you finally stopped hiding the person you already were.

Nobody Talks About This Part

Here is where I am going to say something that might piss you off a little. Being at Effect has benefits. Real, legitimate, genuinely useful benefits that your unconscious mind has been collecting on for years. And until you get honest about what those benefits are, you will keep unconsciously choosing Effect even when every conscious part of you is desperate to change.

Effect protects you from responsibility. If it is not your fault, you cannot fail. If the circumstances are to blame, you never have to look at your own role. If other people are the problem, you never have to be the solution. That is not a weakness. That is a very sophisticated unconscious protection strategy. It made complete sense at some point in your life. It just has terrible ROI as a long-term plan.

Effect also keeps you connected. Shared suffering creates community. Complaining is a bonding ritual. Victimhood can feel like the price of admission to certain relationships and certain rooms. And walking away from Effect can feel terrifyingly like walking away from the people who finally understand you. Your unconscious mind knows this. It has been doing the math on that trade-off for years.

And Effect keeps you from having to change. Even positive change is terrifying to a nervous system wired for familiarity. Staying in Effect means staying in the known. And to your unconscious mind, the known will always feel safer than the unknown, no matter how much the known is quietly destroying you.

This is why telling yourself to just think positively and choose differently has never worked. You cannot override a benefit you have not identified. You cannot let go of something you are pretending you are not holding.

The Time I Stood Up When Everyone Else Sat Down

Let me tell you about the moment I learned what it actually means to live at Cause, at 21 years old, with zero legal experience, and absolutely no idea what I was walking into.

I was working at what turned out to be a deeply toxic company. Illegal practices. Discrimination. Abuse of power. Labor law violations. It was bad. Like, truly, document-everything-and-call-a-lawyer bad.

When a class action lawsuit was filed, eight of us signed on. Eight people with evidence, with receipts, with legitimate grievances. Eight people who were ready to fight.

And then, one by one... they weren't.

As the case stretched on, people started quietly disappearing from the plaintiff list. The company's lawyers were intimidating. The depositions were brutal. The legal fees were mounting. And slowly, my co-plaintiffs started exiting:

"I can't handle the stress."
"I need to focus on finding a new job."
"Maybe it wasn't as bad as I thought."
"I just want to move on with my life."

Three years later, I was the only one left standing.

Twenty-one years old. No legal experience. Going up against a corporation with deep pockets and ruthless lawyers. Everyone told me to take whatever settlement they offered and walk away. And I was terrified. Let's be very clear about that — I was not some fearless crusader. I was scared basically the entire time. And something in me understood that if I didn't see this through, who would?

Here's what Effect thinking would have sounded like at that moment: "This is too hard. They have more money and better lawyers. I'm just one person. Everyone else gave up, so maybe I should, too. This is happening TO me, and I'm powerless."

Here's what Cause thinking actually sounded like: "This is wrong, and I have evidence. I can't control what they do. I can absolutely control what I do. And I am choosing to stand up for what's right regardless of the outcome."

Three years later, just before we were supposed to go to court, they settled — for more than we had ever originally asked for. The lawyers told me later that my refusal to go away is what forced their hand. They knew I wasn't going to be scared off. And they folded.

Being at Cause doesn't mean controlling your circumstances. It means controlling your response to your circumstances. It means choosing your next move instead of just white-knuckling through whatever is happening around you.

The Day I Chose to Stop Being a Victim

Let me tell you about another moment when I realized I was living my entire life in effect, even though I thought I was a strong, independent woman who had her shit together.

It was 2010, and I was sitting in my car in the parking lot of a grocery store, crying over a cup of coffee that I had just spilled all over myself. Not just a little spill - I'm talking about an entire cup of hot coffee covering my lap, my clothes, and the interior of my car.

Here's the thing: I wasn't crying about the coffee.

I was crying because the coffee was just the latest in a series of things that seemed to be "happening to me." My network marketing business was falling apart because my upline had basically pushed me out. My marriage was struggling because my husband and I couldn't agree on anything. My finances were a mess because I was trying to juggle three different income streams and failing at all of them.

Sitting in that parking lot, covered in coffee, I had what alcoholics call a moment of clarity. I suddenly realized that I was telling myself the exact same story about every area of my life:

"This is happening TO me." "It's not fair." "I can't control what other people do." "Why does this always happen to me?"

And at that moment, I had a choice. I could continue feeling sorry for myself and blaming everyone else for my problems. Or I could ask a different question:

"What if none of this is happening TO me? What if it's all happening FOR me?"

That question changed everything. Because the moment I stopped asking "Why me?" and started asking "What now?" I moved from Effect to Cause. And that's when my life started to transform.

The Effect Equation: How Most People Live

When you're living in Effect, your life follows a very predictable pattern. It looks like this:

CIRCUMSTANCE → REACTION → RESULT

Something happens (circumstance), you react to it emotionally (reaction), and you get whatever result that reaction creates (result). You're essentially living your life in response to whatever is happening around you.

People in Effect spend most of their time focused on the circumstance. They analyze it, complain about it, tell stories about it, and try to figure out why it happened. They become experts at explaining their problems and amateurs at solving them.

Effect thinking sounds like: "I can't start my business because I don't have enough money." "I can't lose weight because I don't have time to exercise." "I can't find love because all the good men/women are taken."

"I can't be successful because I didn't go to the right school." "I can't charge more because people won't pay premium prices in my industry."

Notice the pattern? It's always external circumstances that are preventing the person from having what they want. The problem is always "out there" - other people, the economy, their past, their current situation, their lack of resources.

Effect thinking feels powerless because it IS powerless.

When you believe that your results are determined by circumstances outside your control, you have no choice but to wait for those circumstances to change before your life can improve.

And here's the brutal truth: If you're waiting for your circumstances to change before you change, you'll be waiting forever.

The Cause Equation: How Powerful People Live

When you're living at cause, your life follows a completely different pattern:

CIRCUMSTANCE → CHOICE → ACTION → RESULT

The same circumstances happen (because life happens), and instead of reacting emotionally, you pause and make a conscious choice about how to respond. Then you take action based on that choice, which creates your result.

People at Cause spend most of their time focused on their response. They ask better questions: "How can I use this?" "What can I learn from this?" "What opportunity is hidden in this challenge?" "What's my next move?"

Cause thinking sounds like: "I want to start my business, so I'm going to figure out how to start with the resources I have and create more money as I go." "I want to lose weight, so I'm going to find ways to be active that fit into my current schedule and gradually build from there." "I want to find love, so I'm going to become the kind of person who attracts the kind of partner I want." "I want to be successful, so I'm going to leverage my unique background and experiences as advantages." "I want to charge premium prices, so I'm going to position myself as a premium provider and find clients who value quality."

Cause thinking feels powerful because it IS powerful. When you take responsibility for your response to circumstances, you regain control over your results.

The Coffee Spill Rematch (Spoiler: I Won)

Here is something nobody tells you about transformation. It does not always announce itself. It does not always show up as the divorce or the diagnosis or the moment you walk away from everything you built and start over from scratch. Sometimes, and this is the part that will sneak up on you if you are not paying attention, transformation shows up in the completely ordinary, utterly unremarkable moments that you would never put in a highlight reel. The Tuesday morning coffee spill that you laugh off instead of letting ruin your day. The difficult email you respond to with clarity instead of defensiveness. The unexpected setback you pivot around instead of spiraling into. The conversation that could have gone sideways and didn't because you showed up differently than you used to. These are the moments that do not feel significant enough to examine. And they are also, if you know what to look for, the most honest mirror you will ever hold up to yourself. Because how you do the small thing is how you do everything. And when you start noticing that the small things are landing differently, that you are choosing differently, showing up differently, and becoming someone your past self would not even fully recognize, that is when you know the work is not just something you are doing. It is something you are becoming.

So fast forward from that parking lot breakdown to a few years ago when I was teaching one of my masterclasses. I was about halfway through an important presentation when I knocked over an entire cup of coffee, spilling it all over my desk, my computer, my notes, and myself.

Old me (effect mode) would have been mortified. I would have apologized profusely, gotten flustered, and probably cut the training short because I was so embarrassed. I would have spent the rest of the day beating myself up and telling the story of how I "ruined" the presentation.

The new me (cause mode) had a different response.

The moment the coffee spilled, I made a conscious choice: "This is not going to derail me or my participants' experience. I'm going to handle this with grace and keep delivering value."

I calmly moved the electronics away from the spill, grabbed some napkins, and said to my audience, "Well, that's going to be a great example for the blooper reel! Sometimes life gives you unexpected moments to practice staying in cause versus effect. This is cause in action."

I cleaned up what I could, left the rest for later, and continued teaching. My participants later told me that my response to the coffee spill was one of the most powerful demonstrations they'd seen of what it looks like to stay at cause when shit hits the fan.

The first time, the spilled coffee confirmed my victim story and added to my evidence that "things always go wrong for me." The second time, it became a teaching moment that actually enhanced my credibility and connection with my audience.

Your Biology Is Not Your Friend Right Now (Sorry)

Before we talk about how to actually make this shift, I need to give you a reality check on why it's hard, and it has nothing to do with you being weak, broken, or somehow less evolved than the people who seem to do this effortlessly.

It's hard because your biology is working against you. And you deserve to know that.

When something triggers an Effect response, your amygdala fires before you have consciously registered what is happening. Cortisol and adrenaline flood your system in milliseconds. Your prefrontal cortex, the part responsible for rational thought, perspective, creativity, and basically everything that makes you a functioning adult, goes partially offline. This is not a character flaw. This is your nervous system doing exactly what it was designed to do, approximately forty thousand years ago, when threats were actual predators, not difficult Slack messages.

The problem is your nervous system cannot tell the difference between a lion chasing you and a client leaving a bad review. Both trigger the same cascade. Both narrow your vision. Both shove you hard into Effect. And from inside a cortisol flood, you cannot think your way to Cause no matter how many damn personal development books you have read. Your biology simply will not allow it.

So the first move when you feel yourself going into Effect is not to immediately reframe it. It is to regulate your nervous system first. Breathe. Actually breathe, not the shallow "I'm breathing while I panic" breathing. Real breathing. Move your body. Get outside if you can. Give your prefrontal cortex a chance to come back online. You are not failing at your mindset. You are fighting your own biology. Regulate first. Choose second.

How to Actually Make the Shift (For Real, Not Just in Theory)

Once your nervous system is regulated, the shift becomes possible. Here is how it actually works.

Step one is awareness without judgment. You cannot shift from a place you cannot see. Before you can choose Cause you have to be brutally honest about where you are. And most people in Effect do not know they are in Effect. They think they are just being realistic. They think their reaction is completely proportionate. They think they are just telling the truth about what happened. Awareness means being willing to ask one simple question — am I at Cause or in Effect right now? Not to shame yourself. Just to see clearly. You can't change your address if you don't know where you live.

Step two is finding the benefit. Ask yourself what being in Effect is giving you in this specific situation. Safety from responsibility? Belonging through shared complaint? Protection from a change you are not ready for? You need to see the benefit clearly before you can consciously choose to release it. This is not about judging yourself for having it. It is about seeing it so you can decide whether it is still worth the price you are paying.

Step three is shifting your perspective. Effect sees one story. Cause asks for more. What else could this mean? What might I be missing? What would I see if I looked at this from a completely different angle? What does this situation have to teach me that I have been refusing to learn? This is not toxic positivity. This is not slapping a good vibes only sticker on genuine pain and calling it growth. It is being willing to look at the full picture instead of the heavily filtered version your unconscious handed you.

Step four is taking ownership. Not blame. Not shame. Ownership. The question is not whose fault this is. The question is, what is my role in this, and what can I actually do about it? Ownership is where your power lives. Full stop.

Step five is taking inspired action. Not frantic, panicked, oh-crap action born from desperation. Inspired action. The kind that comes when you are regulated and at Cause, and your intuition can actually be heard over the noise. This is where things change. Not in the awareness. In the movement.

A Quick Map So You Know Where You Are

Here is a cheat sheet for identifying in real time which side of the line you are operating from. No judgment. Just information.

Cause - Results	Effect - Excuses
Abundance, gratitude	**Fear, scarcity, and lack**
Intuition	**inner ego, inner child, inner critic**
Inspired action	**Victim of circumstance**
Responsibility	**Blame, shame, justify**
Opportunities	**Assumptions, judgements, interpretations**
Awareness, Learnings	**Limiting decisions & beliefs**
Creativity	**What's not working**
Proactive (possibility)	**Reactionary (necessity)**

Look at that list honestly. Not on your worst day. Not on your best day. On your average Tuesday. Because your average days are what build your life.

Before We Go Into The Tasking

I need to address something directly because this teaching oftentimes gets weaponized, and I refuse to let that happen here.

Being at Cause is not the same as pretending you were not hurt. It is not spiritual bypassing. It is not slapping a gratitude journal on top of genuine pain and calling it transformation. Real things have happened. Those things deserve to be honored, not dismissed. Cause is not about pretending otherwise.

Being at Cause is not the same as never needing support. Trying to think your way out of deep Effect alone is like trying to perform surgery on yourself. Technically possible. Deeply inadvisable. And you're not going to stay conscious long. You cannot always see your own blind spots. You cannot always regulate your own nervous system out of decades of accumulated programming by yourself. That is not a weakness. That is exactly why doing this work with the right support changes everything in a way that solo willpower never will.

And being at Cause is not a permanent achievement you unlock and never lose again. It is a practice. You will slip into Effect. Everyone does. Including me. The goal is not perfection. The goal is to catch yourself faster, spend less time there, and keep building the version of you who chooses Cause more naturally and more quickly every single time.

Cause is not a destination. It is a direction.

And every single time you choose it, you become a little more of the person who chooses it without having to think so damn hard about it.

Now let's do the work.

YOUR CAUSE AND EFFECT AUDIT

Time to get honest about where you're living in effect versus cause. This audit will help you identify the areas where you're giving away your power:

This is your workbook moment. Not later, not after you finish the book, not when you find the perfect pen…now. Open it up, find this section, and do the audit on paper. There is something about writing things down that makes it very difficult to keep pretending you do not know what you know. Which is exactly why most people skip this part. That is also exactly where the gold is. You are not most people. You bought the book. Do the work.

Part 1: Language Audit

Pay attention to your language for one week. Every time you catch yourself using victim language, write it down:

- "I can't..."
- "I have to..."
- "They won't let me..."
- "I don't have a choice..."
- "It's not fair..."
- "Why does this always happen to me?"

For each victim statement, practice reframing it with cause language:

- "I can't" becomes "I'm choosing not to."
- "I have to" becomes "I'm deciding to."
- "They won't let me" becomes "I haven't convinced them yet."
- "I don't have a choice" becomes "I don't like my options, but I still get to choose."

Part 2: Story Audit

What stories are you telling about your life circumstances? Write down the victim story you tell about:

- Your finances
- Your career/business
- Your relationships
- Your health
- Your past

For each victim story, ask yourself:

What would the cause version of this story sound like?

What opportunities am I missing by staying attached to the victim version?

How is this victim story serving me? (Because it is serving you somehow, or you wouldn't keep telling it)

Part 3: Circumstance vs. Choice Audit

List the top 5 things you're currently unhappy about in your life. For each one, ask:

What parts of this situation are truly outside my control (circumstances)?

What parts of this situation are within my control (choices)?

Where am I giving away power by focusing on the circumstances instead of my choices?

Part 4: Responsibility Audit This one might sting, but it's the most important:

Where am I blaming others for my results?

Where am I making excuses instead of taking action?

Where am I waiting for someone else to change before I change?

Where am I using my past as a reason to limit my future?

Living at Cause: The Daily Practice

Shifting from effect to cause isn't a one-time decision. It's a daily practice. Here's how to make it a habit:

Every Morning: "What do I want to create today, and what actions will I take to create it?"

Every Evening: "Where did I give away my power today, and how can I reclaim it tomorrow?"

The goal isn't perfection. Perfection is for people who've never actually lived. The goal is just to catch yourself, mid-blame, mid-spiral, mid-"why does this always happen to me," and choose again. That's it. That's the whole thing.

You are not a victim of your circumstances. You are not powerless. You are not at the mercy of anyone else's choices, baggage, bad behavior, or whatever chaos the universe has been serving up lately.

You are the cause of your life. Full stop. No asterisks. No fine print.

You always have been. You just forgot for a minute.

Now you remember. So what the hell are you waiting for?

CHAPTER 5
THE MAP YOU NEVER HAD

"The only way out is through."
– Robert Frost

Here is something nobody tells you when you decide to change your life.

Deciding to change is the easy part. You have been doing it your whole life. You decided in the shower. You decided at midnight. You decided on a Monday with a new journal and aggressive color-coding. The decision costs you nothing, and it feels incredible… for about four days. And every single time you meant it. Meaning it is not the same as doing it. And deciding is not the same as transforming. What nobody tells you is that the decision is just the entrance. And the entrance is not the transformation. The gap between the moment you decide and the moment you actually are different, that is where most people's dreams go to die. Not because they stopped caring. Because nobody ever gave them the map for what actually lives in that gap.

That map is what you are about to get.

What happens in between is a process. A predictable, reliable, completely non-negotiable process that every single human being who has ever transformed anything has moved through, whether they knew it or not. And the reason most people fail is not that they are weak or lazy or somehow cosmically cursed, it is because they hit a specific stage of this process, decide they are going the wrong direction, and stop.

They reset. They go back to the beginning. They do the whole damn thing over again, wondering why they keep ending up in the exact same place, wearing a slightly different outfit with a fresh new journal.

You are about to stop doing that. Fair warning, though. What you are about to read is going to be uncomfortably specific. You are going to see yourself in places you did not expect to and at volumes you did not ask for. Good.

You Are Not Scared of Success. You Are Not Scared of Failure. You Are Scared of Change. (And Yes, There Is a Difference.)

Before we get into the model, I need to blow up something you have probably been telling yourself for years.

When I ask audiences what they are afraid of, the room splits almost perfectly in half. Half say success. Half say failure. And every single time, someone raises their hand and says both, and everyone else nods like they just heard the most profound and relatable thing in human history.

It is not profound. It is a story.

You are not scared of success. You are not scared of failure. What you are actually scared of, what is quietly running the whole show underneath both of those very convincing narratives, is ***change***.

Because you know the problems you have right now. You know them intimately, like an annoying roommate you have lived with so long that you have memorized their schedule. You know their shape, their rhythm, and exactly how bad they get on a bad day. And your unconscious mind, the part running 95% of everything you do, would rather keep the problems it knows than risk the wide-open terrifying uncertainty of problems it does not.

Known suffering always beats unknown possibility. Every time. Without fail. Your unconscious is not trying to destroy you. It is trying to keep you alive. And from where it is sitting, change looks a lot like a lion, not a teddy bear.

(It's not a lion, and try telling that to the part of your brain that has been running on jungle survival software since before you could walk.)

This is not a character flaw. This is biology doing its job. The Universal Model of Change is the map of how your unconscious navigates this, and I need you to understand something before we go any further. This is not something I pulled out of thin air. This is not something someone came up with in a boardroom to sell you a course. What I call the Universal Model of Change is my way of mapping what decades of behavioral science, from Prochaska and DiClemente's Stages of Change to NLP and researchers on the unconscious mind, have consistently shown about how human beings actually transform.

The pattern was already there. I just gave it a name you can use. And it is what your unconscious mind is already doing right now, today, in your business, your relationships, your bank account, your body. Every single day.

I am just naming it so you can finally stop being ambushed by it.

The Universal Model of Change: A → B → C → D → A'

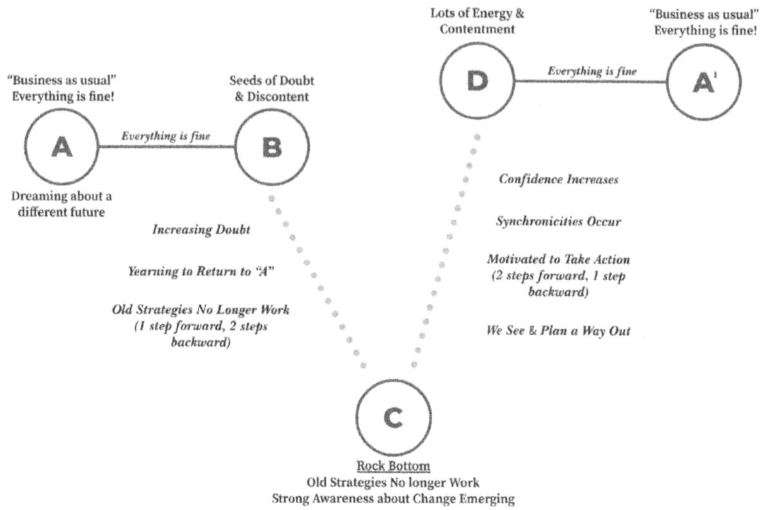

Five stages. Every transformation you have ever made, failed to complete, or are currently spinning your wheels inside of follows this exact path.

No exceptions. No shortcuts. There is no version of this that skips the uncomfortable parts because you are extra motivated this time, and you really, really mean it.

(You always really mean it consciously. That is not the issue. The issue is what comes next.)

Let's walk through it.

Stage A: When Life Is Good

Stage A is good. Let's be really clear about that. Things are working. Your business is moving, your relationships feel solid, and your life has a rhythm that actually feels like yours. You are not white-knuckling it through the day. You are not secretly drowning. You are genuinely, legitimately happy, and that happiness is real. Don't let anyone take that from you.

This matters because most models of change start with pain. They assume you move because something is broken. And that is not always the story. Sometimes change begins not in crisis but in contentment. You are skipping along, life is good, you are grateful for it, and honestly, you should be. And then, almost imperceptibly, something shifts.

A seed lands. It might be a dream you had tucked away in the back of your heart like an old love letter you forgot about. A conversation that stirs something you did not know was still alive in you. A quiet moment where you look at your genuinely good life and feel the first faint pull toward something more. Not because anything is wrong. Just because something in you is waking up and it has opinions. Loud ones. Inconvenient ones. The kind that show up uninvited at 2 am when you were perfectly fine sleeping.

And then the seeds of doubt start to follow. Slowly, not dramatically. The strategies that have always worked start to feel just slightly off. The results that used to come easily require a little more effort. Nothing catastrophic, just a low hum of discontent beneath the surface of a life that still looks completely fine from the outside. Your unconscious is already picking up the signal before your conscious mind even has language for it. Your conscious mind is still waking up, completely unbothered. Adorable.

That is Stage A. Life is good, until it starts quietly and persistently whispering that good might not be the whole story anymore. And that whisper, that sneaky, relentless, won't-shut-up whisper, is what begins to pull you toward Stage B. Buckle up buttercup.

Stage B: When the Discontent Moves In

Stage B is not a moment. It is a mood that becomes a season.

You are still in the life you built. The good one. Yet somewhere between Stage A and right now, the good stopped feeling like enough, and the strategies that used to work have started quietly failing you. The results that came easily now require more effort and deliver less. The relationship that felt solid now feels strained in ways you cannot quite name. The business that was humming now has a rattle in the engine you cannot locate. Nothing is going right. And you cannot figure out why, because you are doing everything you have always done.

Nothing is catastrophically wrong. Nothing feels quite right either.

And here is the worst part. You cannot go back to how things were before the seeds landed, before the doubt crept in. You have seen something you cannot unsee. And believe me, you are going to try. Oh, you are going to try so hard. You are going to lie in bed at 3 am doing a full highlight reel of Stage A like it was the golden era of your life. You are going to romanticize the hell out of it. Remember when things were easy? Remember when the clients came in, and the money flowed, and the relationship felt good, and you did not spend every Sunday with that low-grade existential dread sitting on your chest like a lazy cat? Yeah. You remember. And you want it back so badly you can taste it.

You cannot un-know what you know. You cannot un-feel what you felt. The dream has already landed. The doubt already moved in, and it did not bring an overnight bag; it brought furniture. So you live in the gap. What used to feel like a good life now feels like a comfortable prison, and the bars are made of everything that used to work. The routines. The strategies. The identity you built around the version of you that was thriving in Stage A. Fine, meaning functional. Fine, meaning you know what to expect. Fine, meaning your unconscious has mapped every corner of this place and knows exactly how to run it without asking your conscious mind for permission once.

You built a really nice cage, babe. It's still a cage.

The ceiling is low enough to touch, and you have been standing there so long that you have stopped noticing your neck is bent.

You want the ease of Stage A back. The rhythm of it. The certainty of it. You also know, somewhere underneath all the noise, that something has to change. And that question is exactly where the trouble starts. Because instead of moving forward into something new, most people do something completely understandable and completely costly.

They fucking go back to Stage A and try to do it better.

Honey, no.

The A-B Cycle: The Loop That Spins Faster and Faster

Here is where it gets fucked.

Because here is what most people do when Stage B becomes unbearable. Instead of moving forward into C, into the unknown, into the transformation that is actually waiting for them, they retreat. They go back to Stage A and try to do the same thing with more effort, more conviction, more hustle, more hope. They redecorate the prison instead of leaving it.

That. Is. The. A-B cycle.

Not a dramatic crossroads. Not a moment of clarity with a good soundtrack. Just that quiet, infuriating, completely human loop of "something has to change" followed within five business days with "let me try the thing I already tried, but with more conviction this time."

And here is the part that makes this genuinely brutal. The A-B cycle does not stay at the same speed. It gets faster. And faster. And faster and faster and faster and faster. Until you are spinning so fast you cannot track it anymore. You genuinely believe you are working incredibly hard, because you are. You are just working incredibly hard at going in a very expensive fucking circle.

You know this circle. You have named it. You have journaled about it. You have talked to your friends about it at brunch, over wine, in the parking lot of your therapist's office. And somehow you are still in it. Weird, right? Not weird. It's the cycle. Keep reading.

I know this cycle personally. Not theoretically. Not from a case study I read in a textbook. I lived this. I was in an A-B cycle in my marriage for eight years out of twenty-five. Eight years. Let that sink in. Eight years of everything is fine, things are not great, let's try this, that is not working, let's try couples therapy, nope, okay, he will get help this time, for real this time, he promised this time, that did not work either, let me try yet another approach because apparently I had not suffered enough yet. I kicked him out three times. Three. He came back. I let him.

Because that is what the A-B cycle does to you. It makes you confuse familiarity with hope. We took what was supposed to be our 25th anniversary trip that was really a "can we save this marriage" trip, which is a very expensive way to have the same argument in a prettier location. I even brought him in and did trauma release work with him because I was out of ideas and apparently also out of fucks to give. I decided that if I could just fix him hard enough, everything would be fine.

Spoiler alert. It was not fine.

(And look, I am not going to stand here and pretend I was just an innocent bystander in my own marriage. I had my stuff too. My patterns. My blind spots. The ways I showed up were not exactly a prize either. I was so busy trying to fix him that I did not always look at what I was bringing to the chaos. It takes two people to build a cycle, and I was in there building right alongside him.)

Here is the truth. We were both the problem. I can own my part and still say that out loud without apology.

The cycle was spinning faster and faster. Not because I was stupid. Not because I was not doing the work. Because my identity was not ready to let go of who I had decided I was. I had built myself around being a cop's wife. Around not being another statistic. Around not being one more law enforcement marriage that fell apart. I held onto that identity for dear life because letting it go meant going somewhere my unconscious did not have a single map for. I hadn't decided I was DONE yet.

And that is the whole thing about the A-B cycle that nobody wants to hear. It does not care how tired you are. It does not care how self-aware you are. It does not care how many programs you have bought, how many books you have highlighted, or how many declarations you have made at an appropriate volume with complete sincerity. It will keep running until you get done enough, genuinely, bone-deep, no more negotiating, to stop retreating.

One more thing about this cycle that I need you to tattoo somewhere prominent.

Awareness is not transformation.

Read it again. Slowly this time.

Awareness is not transformation. Awareness is the A-B cycle with better vocabulary. You can be the most self-aware person in every room you walk into and still not change a single damn thing. Because awareness lives in your conscious mind. And the patterns live in your unconscious. Your conscious mind does not have access to where the actual problem is stored.

Understanding why you do the thing does not stop you from doing the thing. Just like knowing exactly how a horror movie ends does not stop you from watching it alone at midnight and then sleeping with the lights on.

The only way out of Stage B is not back. It is forward. Into C.

Stage C: Rock Bottom Is Not What You Think It Is

When most people hear "rock bottom," they picture catastrophe. Losing everything. The diagnosis. The bankruptcy. The relationship is combusting so spectacularly that every option except change gets removed by force. The moment the universe gets so tired of waiting that it picks you up and drops you directly into your C, whether you are ready or not.

That is one version of C. It is not the only one. And sitting around waiting for that version before you permit yourself to transform is one of the stupidest things you will ever do, and you are doing it every single day you stay in the cycle.

C is not rock bottom in the dramatic, lose-everything sense. C is the moment you are done with the stuff that is not serving you. That is the whole definition. The complete one. C is the moment you stop negotiating. Stop trying to go back and do it better. Stop entertaining the voice that says maybe one more try will finally fix the thing that forty-seven fucking tries have not touched.

C is when you get quiet and real and completely, irreversibly finished.

Not "I posted about it" finished. Not "I said it out loud in a group program" finished. Bone-deep, no-more-audience-needed, done-having-this-conversation-with-myself finished.

And here is the truth I want you to sit with until it gets uncomfortable. C is where the transformation actually happens. Not in the reading. Not in the awareness. Not in the intentions, or the journaling, or the program you signed up for that is sitting in your inbox collecting digital dust. In the C. If you do not voluntarily get into your C, if you do not get done enough, real enough, finished enough to stop retreating, the universe will put you there anyway.

It always does. It just does it in ways you would not have chosen for yourself.

I chose my C with cancer.

When I got the diagnosis, I had a choice about how to meet it. I could treat it as something happening to me, (effect, the way we talked about in the last chapter) or I could get into my C with everything I had and do the actual work at the level where it needed to happen. I chose C. I jumped in completely. I did all the steps. I reprogrammed the core program that had been running underneath everything. I did not spend a single minute looking for a way to climb back to B and make something better. I thought about those eight years in the marriage cycle. About how long I had stayed in something that was not working because my identity was not ready to let go. I was not doing that again. Not with this.

And yes, I know some of you are reading that and already plotting your escape route out of C. You are in there right now with your little backpack packed, looking for the ladder. Maybe if I just tweak this one thing. Maybe if I just try that strategy one more time, but harder. Maybe if I read one more book, hire one more coach, and do one more vision board with better fonts. I am going to need you to put the ladder down and back away slowly. That is not C. That is B with a motivational poster on the wall. C does not have a ladder. C has a very clearly marked exit. And the only way out is through.

I got out cancer-free in six months.

I fired THE Stanford Cancer Center and all.

(Yes, really. We will talk about that more. The point right now is this: C works. The only thing C requires is that you actually go there instead of spending your life circling the entrance.)

Now, does C always look like cancer? Absolutely not. Does it always look like losing everything? No. C does not have to be traumatic. C does not have to be the universe dragging you there by the collar. C just has to be real. It just has to be the genuine, no-more-negotiating, I-am-done-having-this-conversation version of finished.

And some of you, bless you, have actually walked right up to the edge of C from B. You have stood there and looked over. You have felt it. You have seen exactly what needs to change and exactly what it is going to cost you. You got close enough to smell it. And then you took one long look down, whispered "absolutely not," and backed slowly away to go try Stage A one more time with a new journal and a fresh set of affirmations. No judgment. Truly. We have all stood at that edge. The view is terrifying. C asks you to let go of things your identity has been gripping onto like a life raft. Your nervous system will throw every excuse it has at you to get you to step back. Not yet. Not like this. Maybe if I just try one more thing first. The edge will be there when you are ready. Just know that waiting for readiness is how people end up letting the universe decide for them. And the universe is not known for its subtlety.

There is no way around it. There is no shortcut from B to D. I know you want there to be. I know some of you are already looking for it. Maybe if I just do enough mindset work. Maybe if I just find the right strategy.

Maybe if I read enough books and attend enough seminars and visualize hard enough, I can skip straight to the good part.

You cannot. No exceptions. Nobody gets to go from B to D. The only path to D runs directly through C. Through the discomfort. Through the identity shed. Through the terrifying, necessary, completely non-negotiable act of becoming the 'Not Me'. There is no tunnel around it, no bridge over it, no way to MacGyver your way past it with enough hustle and enough strategy and enough sheer fucking determination. C is not an obstacle between you and your transformation. C is the transformation. It is the whole thing. It is where the actual work happens at the actual level where it needs to happen.

C is not a choice. C is a destination. The only thing that is actually up for debate is whether you arrive there on your own terms, with your bag packed and your eyes open, or whether the universe eventually loses patience and kicks your ass through the door in the most inconvenient, dramatic, and expensive way it can think of. Everyone gets to C. The only real question is whether you went in like a decision or got sent in like a consequence.

What C Actually Looks Like: Becoming the Not Me

Here is what C is actually asking you to do.

C is asking you to become the 'Not Me'.

Not a better version of the current you. Not the current you with upgraded habits and a morning routine. The actual, full, terrifying, unfamiliar version of you that you have been hiding from. The one that requires you to shed the identity you have been gripping like it is the only thing keeping you alive. The one that feels dangerous and uncertain and foreign and nothing like the self your unconscious has spent years making safe.

Albert Einstein said you cannot solve a problem with the same mind that created it. That is the A-B cycle in one sentence. You cannot think your way out using the thinking that got you in. You cannot strategize your way into a new life using the strategies built by the old version of you.

The mind that created the problem is the problem. Which means the solution is not a better plan. The solution is a different you.

True transformation is not addition. It is not adding new habits onto the old identity like a fresh coat of paint on a rotting wall. It is a full identity shed. It is looking at the version of yourself that has been running the show and saying, with love and without apology, that this is not who I am anymore. It is building a new version of safety from scratch, because the old version of safety is exactly what has been keeping you stuck.

And yes, that is terrifying. The new version of you feels uncertain. Unfamiliar. Like trying to walk in heels on a cobblestone street. Technically possible. Deeply uncomfortable. Worth it when you get where you are going. Your nervous system is going to throw every alarm it has at you because unfamiliarity reads as danger, even when it is actually freedom.

And that uncertain, scary, not-yet-solid version of you? That is the one who gets the results. That is the one standing on the other side of everything you say you want.

C is where the old strategies are done. Where a new identity is being forced to the surface, whether you cooperate with it or not. And the only direction that leads anywhere worth going is through. Not back. Not around. Through.

Stop. Climbing. Backwards.

Being inside your C comes with a built-in problem that has nothing to do with how smart or self-aware you are. You cannot read the label from inside the jar. You are too close to it, too identified with it, too thoroughly inside it to see what is actually running. You will try. You will journal and reflect and analyze, and you will get impressively close. But the pattern keeping you stuck is invisible to the eye.

This is why the 'Not Me' cannot be found alone. You cannot see your own blind spots. You cannot break a pattern you cannot see. And you cannot become a version of yourself that your current identity does not yet recognize as possible. That requires someone outside the jar.

Someone who can see what you cannot, name what you have been looking at your whole life, and help you clear it at the level where it actually lives, not manage it from the surface, actually clear it permanently.

When are you going to be done? Not when will you feel ready? Ready is not coming. Ready is the story B tells you in order to keep you in B. When are you going to be done?

Stage D: Baby Giraffe Legs and the Life You Actually Came Here For

You made it through C. The core program shifted. The old identity is done. And now you are standing on the other side, going, "what the actual hell just happened," and also "oh my god, is this real," and also "why am I crying in the grocery store?"

Welcome to Stage D. You absolute badass. You did it.

Let that land for a second because you deserve it. You looked at the thing. You went into the thing. You did not climb back up to B and redecorate. You went through. And now you are here, on the other side, at the end of the rainbow, the pot of gold is real, and it is yours, and you earned every single ounce of it.

This is the stage nobody talks about enough because everyone is so focused on surviving C that they forget to tell you how freaking spectacular D actually is. So let's talk about it.

In Stage D, your confidence starts to climb in a way that feels almost suspicious. Like you keep waiting for someone to tap you on the shoulder and tell you there has been a mistake. Opportunities start showing up that would have blown right past the old version of you. Synchronicities start happening so fast that you cannot keep up with them. You will bump into the exact right person at the exact right moment. The thing you needed will appear before you even finish asking for it. The universe, which has been waiting very patiently for you to get your shit together, is now fully cooperating with the new version of you, and it is showing off a little.

Your energy is back. Not the frantic, white-knuckling, forcing-it energy of the A-B cycle. Real energy. Clean energy. The kind that comes from finally moving in the right direction instead of just moving fast. You wake up, and things feel possible in a way they did not before. You are using new strategies, and they are actually working, so you keep looking around like, "Who is this person, and where has she been because she is incredible?"

The new identity is real. It's yours. And it is exciting in the way that only brand new things can be exciting, full of possibility, full of momentum, full of the specific joy that comes from finally, finally, finally becoming the version of yourself you always knew was in there.

You also are a baby giraffe.

You made it through C. The core program shifted. The old identity is done. And now you are in Stage D, you feel like an absolute stranger in your own life. You are the new version of you, and you have not quite figured out how to walk yet. You are looking around, going: "Okay. Is this actually real? Am I going to be able to handle this? What if I accidentally go back into my C?" Every step feels uncertain. The new identity exists, it's real, it's yours, and it does not feel automatic yet. You are learning to operate a version of yourself that fits better than the old one, but whose mechanics you have not fully mastered.

This is completely normal. This is exactly what it is supposed to look like. A baby giraffe does not decide the wobble means it's not meant to walk. It falls, and it gets up, and it falls, and it gets up, and one day getting up is just what it does without thinking. You are doing the same thing in a slightly less adorable way.

Unfortunately, here is where Stage D gets dangerous. Because it feels uncertain and unfamiliar, a lot of people start interpreting the wobble as evidence that the transformation was not real. The old thoughts surface. The old feelings come back for a visit like that one guest who did not get the memo that the party is over. The old patterns try to run one more time like a finale nobody asked for. And the Inner Critic, who has been suspiciously quiet during the work, suddenly has a lot of very compelling opinions about how maybe the old identity was not so bad after all.

Do not listen to it. That voice is basically your inner critic doing one final audition for a role it already lost. You did the work. You cleared the thing. You became someone your old self would be absolutely gobsmacked by. The wobble is not a sign you are falling; it is just what it feels like to walk on new legs in a new life. Baby giraffe, remember? You are going to figure out how to walk. You already are, so keep going.

This is the stage where the new identity needs to be reinforced, tested under real conditions, and protected from the extremely convincing voice that has been running things for a very long time and is not at all pleased about the restructuring. Surround yourself with people who are already living where you just arrived. People for whom what still feels uncertain to you is just Wednesday for them. Their everyday becomes your evidence that everything you thought was impossible is actually just new.

You made it to D. Welcome to the other side. Now go enjoy the damn view.

Stage A': The New Normal, And Then the Whole Glorious Infuriating Thing Starts Again

You did it. You actually did it.

Stage A' (A Prime) is what you have been working toward. The new normal. The upgraded life. The version of you that the old you would have looked at with her jaw on the floor, going "wait, that is actually me?" Yes. That is actually you. She is incredible. And she has absolutely earned the right to enjoy this.

Things are working. Really working. The kind of work that feels almost suspicious because you spent so long grinding, that ease feels like a trick. It is not a trick. This is just what life looks like when you are finally operating from the right identity.

The pricing conversation you used to rehearse for three days, lying awake at 2 am running through every possible response, happens in the moment now. Clean. Confident. Done. You move on with your life like it was nothing because for the new version of you, it actually is nothing. Saying no, the kind that used to require a week of preparation, a therapy session, and a three-day guilt hangover, now just comes out clean. The decision that used to spiral you for three weeks gets made on a Tuesday. Before lunch. The internal committee that used to convene every time you needed to do something brave has been disbanded. Permanently. You didn't even have to send a formal notice.

You are skipping along. Life is genuinely, legitimately good. You are grateful for it, and you should be because you went through some serious shit to get here. You earned every bit of this. Soak it in.

And then…

You already know what happens next, don't you? Because you have been here before, just at a lower level. A seed lands. A quiet pull toward something more. A dream that feels bigger than the current version of big. A moment where you look at your genuinely incredible life and feel that familiar, inconvenient, 2 am whisper that there might be even more available.

Oh, for the love of all that is fucking holy!

Welcome to spiral dynamics. Stage A' is your new Stage A. The new normal becomes the new comfort zone. The strategies that got you here start to feel just slightly off. The results that came easily start requiring a little more effort. And somewhere in the back of your mind, underneath all the contentment and confidence and hard-won peace, a seed is already landing.

This is not a problem. This is the design. This is how growth actually works, not a straight line up, not a destination you arrive at and unpack your bags, but a spiral. Always moving upward. Each cycle builds on the last. Each transformation makes the next one faster and less terrifying because you have the receipts now. You have been through your C before. You know what it produces. You know what is waiting on the other side.

And every version of you has been better than the last one.

Every. Single. One.

The difference between Stage A and Stage A' is not just the level. It is the knowing. You are not starting from scratch. You are starting from experience. From evidence. From the lived, bone-deep, can-not-be-taken-from-you knowledge that you have done hard things before and come out the other side better than you went in. The new B will still be uncomfortable. The new C will still ask you to shed an identity. And you know the process. You have the map. You have the tools.

The longer you do this work, the less terrifying C becomes. Not because C gets easier. It's because you know what it is. You know what it produces. And you know that every single time you have come out the other side, you have looked back at the version of you who was terrified to go in and thought, "Oh sweetheart, if you only knew what was waiting."

You already know how to do this. You have always known how to do this.

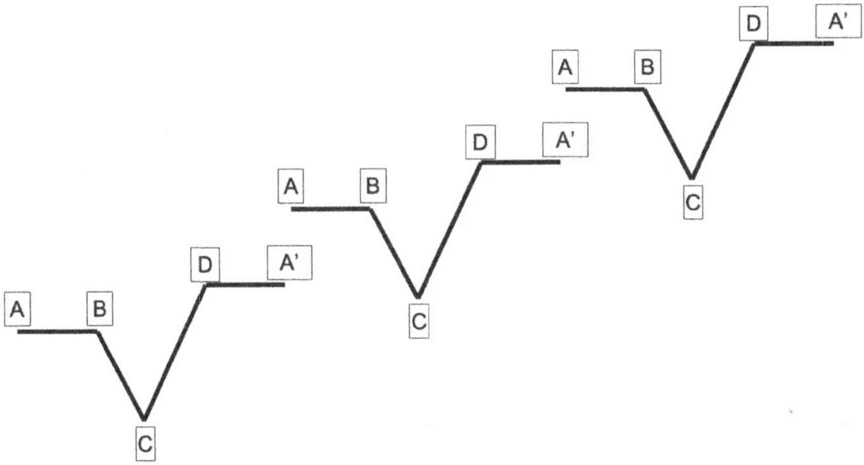

So Where the Hell Are You Right Now

Not rhetorically. Actually. Put down your defenses for thirty seconds and actually answer this. No performance. No curated self-awareness. Just the real answer, the one you already know, the one that has been sitting in your chest this whole chapter, waiting for you to stop scrolling past it.

Are you in Stage A, life is genuinely good, things are working, you are grateful and happy, and skipping along, but somewhere underneath all that goodness, a seed has already landed, and that inconvenient little whisper has started? The one that shows up uninvited at 2 am when you were perfectly fine sleeping? Have you been calling that whisper "anxiety" or "perfectionism" or "just being someone who wants a lot" when it is actually the next version of you knocking on the door with an overnight bag and very strong opinions?

Are you in Stage B, living in the gap, yearning for the ease of Stage A while knowing you cannot go back, nothing is catastrophically wrong, but nothing feels quite right either, the strategies that used to work are not working anymore, and you cannot figure out why, because you are doing everything you have always done? Have you redecorated the prison so many times that it almost feels like home? Are you standing in a cage you built yourself, touching the ceiling with your neck bent, and calling it fine?

Are you spinning in the A-B cycle, faster and faster, working incredibly hard, genuinely trying, ending up in the same place, carrying a very convincing and extremely well-rehearsed story about why each retreat was actually the strategically reasonable choice given the circumstances at the time?

It was not the strategically reasonable choice. It was the scared choice. There is a difference, and you know it.

Are you standing at the edge of B looking down into your C, going "yeah, no, I'm good, I don't actually need to go down there" while your results are quietly, patiently, relentlessly accumulating evidence that you absolutely do? Have you looked over the edge, felt it, seen exactly what needs to change, and then backed slowly away to go try Stage B one more time with a new journal and a fresh set of affirmations? The edge will be there when you are ready. And you know the universe is there waiting, slightly more impatiently.

Are you already in your C, in the thick of it, old strategies done, new identity not yet solid, trying to climb back up to B with only your elbows, exhausted and confused? You are being asked to become the Not Me. The version of yourself you have been hiding from. The one that feels scary and uncertain and nothing like the self your unconscious has spent years making safe. That version of you is not a threat. That version of you is the whole damn point.

Are you in Stage D on baby giraffe legs, the new version of yourself emerging, uncertain, occasionally ambushed by the old version, the Inner Critic staging one last dramatic comeback performance nobody asked for, needing someone to hold the space while you figure out how to walk in a life that finally fits? Because if you are, I need you to hear this. The wobble is not a warning. The wobble is evidence that you are walking on new ground, you absolute legend!

Or, are you settling into A', a new normal, taking root, things working in that clean, effortless way that still feels slightly suspicious, the next seed already quietly landing, equal parts genuinely excited and already slightly tired at the thought of another cycle? Good. That means you know how this works now. And knowing how it works is the whole game.

Wherever you are is exactly where this work begins. The only wrong answer is the dishonest one. And I say that knowing the dishonest answer is very tempting right now because some of you just located yourself somewhere in this chapter that is significantly more uncomfortable than where you thought you were five minutes ago.

Now, here is what I need you to understand before we go any further.

You have been doing this your entire life.

Every single cycle. Every A, every B, every C, every D, every A'. You have been living this model on repeat since the day you were born. The difference is that until right now, you were doing it completely in the dark. No map. No names for any of it. No way to see the pattern because you were inside it, stumbling through it, being dragged through it, white-knuckling your way through it, and calling it just life. The universe was in the driver's seat, foot on the gas, no GPS, no seatbelts, absolutely no interest in your comfort level, barreling through your life at full speed while you sat in the back seat, blindfolded, holding on for dear life, wondering why everything felt so chaotic and out of control.

That was not your fault. You did not have the map.

You have the map now.

That changes everything. Because having the map actually means you have your hands on the wheel for the first time. It means you are no longer at the mercy of the universe deciding when your C arrives and how hard it hits. It means you can see the A-B cycle the second it starts spinning and call it by its name instead of spending eight years inside it, wondering why nothing is working. It means when you feel the seeds of doubt landing in your beautiful Stage A, instead of being blindsided by it, you can look at it and say, "Oh, I know exactly what this is," and decide consciously what you want to do next.

It means C is no longer an ambush. It is a choice.

And when C is a choice, everything changes. You can jump in with both feet instead of being dragged in sideways. You can do the work at the level where it actually lives instead of spending years managing symptoms on the surface. You can get through it faster, cleaner, with support, with the light on the other side fully visible the entire time. Because you have been through it before. You have the receipts. You know what is waiting, and it is so much better than where you are standing right now.

And then D becomes a landing pad instead of a plot twist. And A' becomes a launchpad instead of a surprise. And then the whole beautiful, infuriating, glorious cycle starts again, except this time you are not a passenger. You are the driver. Fully conscious, fully awake, fully aware, doing this on purpose, going faster and farther than you ever thought possible because you are finally working with the process instead of being worked over by it.

This is what it looks like to grow on your terms.

This is what it looks like to stop being the person things happen to and start being the person who decides.

You have always been doing this. You just could not see it. Now you can. And now that you can see it, you cannot unsee it. Which means the only question left is the one I am going to ask you one more time.

What are you going to do with it?

The One Thing I Actually Need You to Take From This Chapter

C is not punishment. C is not evidence that you made a mistake or chose wrong, or that you are somehow not built for the level you are after.

Let's talk about what actually is dangerous. Because I have watched people read about C and decide it is the scariest part of this whole model. And I need to lovingly, firmly, with absolutely zero apology, tell you that you are looking at the wrong thing.

C is not the dangerous part.

The A-B cycle is the dangerous part.

And here is the thing that is going to make your brain hurt a little. Most people who think they are in their C are not in their C. They are in the A-B cycle, and it has gotten so fast and so exhausting and so relentless that it feels like rock bottom. It feels like everything is falling apart. It feels like nothing is working and nothing will ever work, and maybe this is just who they are, and maybe this is just how life is. And they call that their C.

It is not their C. It is the spin. It is the cycle doing what the cycle does, getting faster and faster and more exhausting until you cannot tell which way is up anymore. That is not a transformation. That is the A-B cycle in its final form before it either breaks you or you break it.

Here is how you know the difference. In the A-B cycle, nothing is working, and you keep trying anyway. You keep going back. You keep tweaking and adjusting and reframing and relaunching and white-knuckling and hoping that this time, with this strategy, with this level of commitment, something will finally shift. You are still in it. You are still fighting for the old version of your life. You are still trying to make A work.

True C is when you are done trying to make A work. Not tired. Not frustrated. Not temporarily defeated before the next relaunch. Done. Bone-deep, no-more-negotiating, I-cannot-do-this-one-more-time done. True C is when the old strategies are not just failing, they are finished. When going back to A is no longer an option, your body will even entertain. When the only direction that makes any sense at all is through.

And that is exactly where most people stop.

Because here is the part nobody wants to say out loud. Most people do not actually want to change. They want the results of change without the transformation that produces them. They want D without C. They want A' without shedding the identity that belongs to A. They walk right up to the edge of true C, the real thing, the actual transformation, and they stop. Every single time. And then they go back to the A-B cycle. Which, let's be clear, is the actual terrifying thing. Not C. C is the door out. The A-B cycle is the room you stay trapped in forever because you were too afraid to open it.

That is the part people avoid. That is the part that keeps people spinning in the A-B cycle for years, for decades, calling it growth while never actually growing.

The A-B cycle will let you feel like you are doing the work. It will let you stay busy enough and self-aware enough and invested enough to feel like change is happening. It will give you enough small wins and enough almost-breakthroughs and enough "I really feel like I am on the edge of something" moments to keep you coming back. And it will take everything you have, your time, your money, your energy, your hope, and give you right back to where you started. Just more tired and with a better story about why.

That is the dangerous part. Not C.

C has an exit. C has a D waiting on the other side with baby giraffe legs and synchronicities and a version of you that your current self cannot fully imagine yet. C is a transformation wrapped in discomfort, and yes, it is scary, and yes, it asks everything of you, and it has a destination. It goes somewhere. It produces something. It changes you at the level where change actually sticks.

So no, C is not the part to be afraid of. The A-B cycle is the part to be afraid of. C is the part to run toward. Because the only thing on the other side of it is everything you have been saying you want.

You have been in your C before. You did not always know that's what it was, and you made it through. Every single time. You got to A' levels, your previous self could not have imagined from where she was standing. You already know how to do this.

Actually transform. Actually shed. Actually, change at the level where change is real and permanent, and nobody can ever take it from you because it is not something you did, it is something you became.

That is everything.

If you are serious about changing your life, you will find a way.

If you are not, you will find an excuse. A very well-reasoned, thoroughly workshopped, completely convincing excuse that your unconscious has been preparing for years and can deliver on demand without breaking a sweat.

Stop retreating. Stop spinning. Stop redecorating the prison.

Go through.

Where The Hell Are You

You just got the thing most people spend their whole lives without, a way to see exactly what has been happening to them and why. You have the names now. You have the model. And now we are going to get ruthlessly, uncomfortably, specifically honest about where you are inside it. Workbook out. Not later. Right now. Because understanding this without doing the work is just a more sophisticated way of staying exactly where you are.

STEP 1: LOCATE YOURSELF. NO LYING TO YOURSELF.

Circle the most honest answer. Not the most flattering one. Not the one that lets you off the hook at the end of the chapter. Not the one your inner committee voted on after a very lengthy and defensive deliberation. The true one.

Stage A — Life is genuinely good. Things are working. You are happy, you are grateful, and you have earned every bit of it. Soak it in. This stage is real, and it is beautiful, and it deserves to be celebrated. And then, right when things are humming along at their best, quietly and without drama, a seed lands. A whisper. A pull toward something more that has nothing to do with being ungrateful and everything to do with the fact that you are someone who keeps growing. That is not a problem. That is just the next version of you introducing yourself.

Stage B — Life is no longer the good thing it was, and you know it. The strategies that used to work are not working anymore. The results that used to come easily now require more effort and deliver less. Nothing is catastrophically wrong, and nothing feels quite right either, and you cannot remember the last time it did. You are living in the gap between the life that used to feel good and a future you cannot fully see yet. You are yearning for the ease of Stage A, like it was the golden era of your life, and you are doing the full highlight reel at 3 am. You want it back so badly you can taste it. But you cannot go back. The seed already landed. The doubt already moved in and brought furniture. You are standing in a cage made of everything that used to work, touching the ceiling with your neck bent, and calling it fine. It is not fine. And some part of you has known that for a while now.

The A-B Cycle — Spinning. Faster and faster. Working incredibly hard at going in a very expensive circle. Nothing is going right, and you cannot figure out why because you are doing everything you have always done. You keep going back to Stage A to try to do the same thing better, and it keeps not working, and you keep going back anyway. You have named this circle. You have journaled about it. You have talked about it at brunch. And somehow here you still are. This, not C, is the dangerous one. This is the one that will eat your entire life if you let it.

Mistaking the A-B Cycle for C — Everything feels like it is falling apart, and you have decided this must be your C. It is not. Nothing is working, but you are still trying to make A work. You are still going back. You are still tweaking and relaunching and hoping this time will be different. That is not a transformation. That is the spin in its most exhausting form. True C has not arrived yet because you are not done yet. And some part of you knows that.

True C — You are done. Not tired. Not temporarily defeated before the next relaunch. Done. Bone-deep, no-more-negotiating, I-cannot-do-this-one-more-time done. The old strategies are finished. Going back to A is no longer something your body will even consider. You are being asked to become the 'Not Me', and everything in you is terrified, and you are doing it anyway. This is not failure. This is the only place transformation has ever actually happened for anyone in the history of change. Stop climbing backward.

Stage D — Baby Giraffe Legs — You made it through C, you absolute legend, and I need you to celebrate that for a second before we move on. The new version of you is here. She is real, and she is yours, and she is learning how to walk. Things are working in ways that feel almost too good to be true; they are not. This is just what the other side actually looks like. Synchronicities are showing up. Confidence is building. The wobble is not a warning. It is the sound of new legs on new ground. Keep going. It only gets better from here.

Stage A' — This is what you were working toward. The new normal. The upgraded life. The version of you that your old self would have looked at with her jaw on the floor, going 'wait, is that actually me?' Yes. That is actually you. Things are flowing in a way that might still feel slightly suspicious; that is just what life looks like when you are finally operating from the right identity. You went through some serious stuff to get here. Soak it in. And then right on schedule, quietly and without drama, a seed lands. The next version of you is already introducing herself. This time, you know exactly what to do.

STEP 2: GET BRUTALLY, UNCOMFORTABLY, SPECIFICALLY HONEST ABOUT WHAT THIS IS ACTUALLY COSTING YOU

I know. You want to skip this part. Every single person who has ever done this work wants to skip this part. It is uncomfortable and inconvenient and requires you to look at numbers, timelines, and truths you have been very skillfully avoiding. Do it anyway. The A-B cycle does not just cost you results. It costs you time you are not getting back. Ever. Not one single day of it. It costs you the version of your life that has been sitting on the other side of the C you have been avoiding, fully furnished, fully waiting, collecting dust while you spin.

Get specific. Get uncomfortable. Get honest. Nobody is grading this except you and the universe, and the universe already knows.

What is your current stage costing you?

In your business or career. In your relationships. In you finances. In your health or energy. In your sense of self. The honest number of months or years you have been here, and let's not round down.

STEP 3: NAME THE DAMN CYCLE

If you are in the A-B cycle, and be honest, because most people are even when they are absolutely convinced they are not, write out your specific version of it. Not the concept. Not the sanitized coaching-speak version. Your actual loop. The specific thing you keep trying. The specific way you keep retreating. The specific story you have been telling yourself about why going back to B was actually the mature, strategic, completely reasonable adult decision given the circumstances at the time.

It was not. And let's hear it anyway.

What does your A-B cycle look like?

What is the story you tell yourself to make going back to A sound reasonable and frankly impressive?

What is the thing you already know you need to do that you stop yourself just before every single time?

STEP 4: DECIDE. RIGHT NOW. NOT LATER. NOW.

You now know more about your own patterns than most people will ever know in a lifetime. You know the cycle. You know the stages. You know which one you are in and what it has been costing you.

Awareness is not transformation. You know that too.

So here is the only question left.

Are you done?

Write it. By hand. Say it out loud if you can.

'I am done with ________. I am choosing my C on my terms before the universe chooses it for me. And I am not climbing back.'

That is not a journal prompt. That is a decision.

Go. Through.

CHAPTER 6
THE POWER OF PLAYING BIG: STOP APOLOGIZING FOR YOUR GENIUS

"I am not afraid of storms, for I am learning how to sail my ship."
— Louisa May Alcott

You were born to be a force of nature. Not a gentle breeze. Not a light drizzle. A full-blown hurricane that changes everything in its path.

And somewhere along the way, you learned to be a whisper instead of a roar. You learned to apologize for taking up oxygen, for having the audacity to be brilliant, for being too much, too loud, too successful, too goddamn amazing for other people's comfort.

You learned to play small.

And playing small is killing your soul one apologetic smile at a time.

I'm not talking about being a humble, kind human here. I'm talking about the soul-crushing habit of dimming your light so other people don't have to squint. I'm talking about making yourself smaller so everyone else can feel bigger. I'm talking about apologizing for being extraordinary when extraordinary is exactly what this world desperately needs.

I'm talking about that voice in your head that sounds like every person who ever told you to: "Sit down and shut up." "Don't get too big for your britches." "Stay in your lane." "Know your place." "Don't rock the boat."

Fuck that voice. And fuck everyone who installed it in your head.

Because the world has enough mediocre people playing it safe and staying small. What the world needs is YOU, at full volume, full power, taking up every inch of space you deserve and then some.

I Discovered My Inner Hurricane

Let me tell you about the moment I realized I had been living as a gentle breeze when I was actually a category-five hurricane.

It was 2017, and I was standing in front of a room of 50 people who had paid thousands of dollars to attend an "X" transformational event. I'll keep it unnamed to protect the innocent. My boss, Marcus, had walked out at lunch on day one, claiming he had a "103-degree fever" and then informed me to "figure it out and make sure you make sales."

Translation: "Handle this shit so I don't have to, and I'll still take credit for any success."

The old me, the playing-small, apologetic, "I'm not qualified" me, would have called him in a panic, begged him to come back, or found some way to deflect responsibility onto someone else.

And just standing there, looking at 50 expectant faces, something inside me snapped. Not in a bad way. In a "holy shit, I'm done pretending I don't know what I'm doing" way.

My intuition, that badass inner voice that never lies, said loud and clear: "Girl, you've been running these events better than him for months. Stop waiting for permission to be brilliant and just BE brilliant."

So I looked at those 50 people and said, "I'm about to blow your fucking minds with the most transformational four days of your life. This is what I was born to do, and you are about to experience exactly why!"

I proceeded to deliver exactly that.

No apologies. No disclaimers. No "I'm just filling in" bullshit. I owned that room like I had been born to stand in front of it.

That event became the highest-rated event in the company's history, and the next event had 100 people. Not because I suddenly developed new skills, but because I finally stopped apologizing for the skills I'd always had.

And here's the real kicker: When Marcus came back and heard about the success, instead of congratulating me, he said, "Don't let it go to your head. You were just following my system."

Even when I played big and got extraordinary results, the people around me were still invested in keeping me small.

That's when I realized playing small isn't just about your own insecurities.

It's about the fact that your bigness threatens people who have built their entire identity around being bigger than you.

The Expensive Education of Playing Small

I got my PhD in playing small from the University of Life, and let me tell you, tuition was a bitch.

I learned to play small before I could even pronounce the word "extraordinary." It started with all the greatest hits:

"Use your inside voice." (Translation: Your natural volume is too much.) "Don't be a show-off." (Translation: Your talents make other people uncomfortable.) "Good girls don't brag." (Translation: Celebrating your wins is unseemly.) "Stay humble." (Translation: Your confidence threatens our need to feel superior.)

By the time I was an adult, I was a fucking master at making myself smaller. I could apologize for breathing if the situation called for it.

In my wedding consulting business, I'd undercharge because I didn't want to seem "money-hungry." (God forbid I should want to make a living from my expertise.)

In my network marketing business, I'd downplay my success because I didn't want my team to feel bad. (Because apparently my job was to manage everyone else's feelings about my achievements.)

In my coaching business, I'd deflect compliments faster than Neo dodging bullets in *The Matrix*.

I was so good at playing small that I could be the most successful person in the room while making everyone else feel like they were more important than me.

I was a goddamn small-playing virtuoso.

And it was costing me everything.

The Nine-Months-Pregnant Power Move

One of my favorite "fuck playing small" moments happened when I was nine months pregnant with my second daughter.

I had earned the right to walk across the stage at the Pre-Paid Legal Services convention in Las Vegas, an event with 50,000 people in attendance. This was the highest recognition in the company, and I had worked my ass off to qualify for it.

The convention was scheduled for two weeks before my due date.

Every logical person in my life lost their damn minds: "You can't travel that pregnant!" "What if you go into labor in Vegas?" "Just skip it this year!" "It's not worth the risk!"

And you know what? I had spent my entire pregnancy building a business while growing a human. I had hit every single qualification while dealing with morning sickness, exhaustion, and all the other joys of pregnancy.

I had earned that moment, and I wasn't about to let it pass because other people were uncomfortable with my big, pregnant, successful self.

So I got on a fucking plane at eight and a half months pregnant and flew to Las Vegas.

When they called my name to walk across that stage, I didn't waddle apologetically. I didn't make self-deprecating jokes about being the size of a house. I didn't diminish the moment.

I waddled across that stage like the badass entrepreneur I was, pregnant belly leading the way, and I owned every second of it.

Fifty thousand people gave me a standing ovation, not just for my business success, but also for showing up fully, unapologetically, taking up space without asking permission.

Two weeks later, I gave birth to my daughter. And I realized that walking across that stage wasn't just about business recognition. It was about modeling for my unborn and 3-year-old daughters, what it looks like to claim your space in the world without apologizing for existing.

The Partnership That Tried to Cage My Hurricane

Want to know how expensive playing small can be? Let me tell you about Sarah, my former business partner.

Sarah was talented at graphic design and web development. I was a fucking sales machine with serious strategic chops. We should have been an unstoppable force.

Unfortunately, Sarah had an unconscious investment in keeping me small.

Every time I'd suggest expanding our services, "That sounds too complicated." Every time I wanted to raise our prices, "We'll lose clients." Every time I'd get excited about new opportunities: "Let's not get ahead of ourselves." Every time I'd close a big sale: "Great, now I have to do all this extra work."

I started second-guessing my instincts. I started apologizing for bringing in business. I started playing smaller and smaller until I was practically invisible in my own company.

The more I played small, the more resentful I became. And the more resentful I became, the more our partnership fell apart.

The whole thing ended when I went to Hawaii for two weeks and came back to discover that Sarah had hired her brother to audit our books, declared that I was "overpaid," cleaned out our business account, and moved to Arizona.

And here's the real lesson: Sarah didn't steal my business because she was evil. She stole it because she couldn't handle me playing big.

My enthusiasm threatened her. My sales success held up a mirror she did not want to look into. My vision for growth asked more of her than she was willing to give.

Instead of rising to meet my energy, she chose to eliminate the source of her discomfort. Me.

That betrayal could have taught me to play even smaller, to be even more apologetic about my gifts.

Instead, it taught me that some people will always be threatened by your magnificence. And those people can fuck right off.

Sarah tried to cage my hurricane. What she did not know, what I did not fully understand yet either, was that you cannot cage a hurricane. You can only delay it. And while I was busy rebuilding from the financial wreckage of that partnership, my body had been quietly keeping score of every moment I had spent making myself smaller than I was. Soon, it was about to send me a message I could not ignore.

What Your Body Has Been Trying to Tell You

Here is something nobody in a doctor's office will ever sit down and explain to you, so I will.

Your body is not the fixed, permanent, set-in-stone thing you have been treating it like. It is rebuilding itself every single day, constantly, relentlessly, whether you are paying attention or not. Scientists at the Weizmann Institute of Science confirmed that roughly 330 billion cells are replaced in the human body every single day. That is approximately one percent of all your cells, gone and rebuilt, before you even finish your morning coffee. The cells lining your stomach and intestines last around five days. Your skin replaces itself every two to four weeks. Your bones take a full ten years to complete their renewal cycle. Research published by Jonas Frisén in 2005, based on carbon dating, showed that the average age of a cell in the human body sits somewhere between seven and ten years.

You are simultaneously ancient and completely new. Which means the story you have been telling yourself about being fixed, finished, and fundamentally incapable of change is not just emotionally untrue.

It is biologically false.

Your body is creating a new version of you right now, in this moment, while you sit here reading this sentence. So that begs the question: what are you programming those new cells with?

Because here's what most people are never taught: dis-ease doesn't just randomly appear in your body. It often traces back to what is called an UDIN event, an experience that was Unexpected, Dramatic, Isolating, and left you with No strategy for how to respond.

A UDIN event is the moment your nervous system got hit so hard, so fast, and so alone that it had no framework for processing what just happened. Your body filed it under "emergency still unresolved" and started holding it. Not metaphorically. Physically. In your tissues. In your nervous system. In the patterns it uses to run your health, your hormones, your immune response, and your energy.

UDIN events can be the obvious ones: a sudden loss, a betrayal, a diagnosis, an accident. They can also be things that looked small from the outside and felt catastrophic on the inside. Being publicly humiliated in third grade. The night your parents had the fight that changed everything. The moment you understood that love in your family came with conditions. Your nervous system does not grade these events by how dramatic they look to other people. It grades them by how alone and unprepared you were when they hit.

Unresolved UDIN events don't just go away. They compound. They stack. They show up as the anxiety you can't explain, the tension you carry in your shoulders, the autoimmune issues that started after the year everything fell apart, the exhaustion that doesn't lift no matter how much you sleep.

Your body keeps the score of every unprocessed emotion, every betrayal you stuffed down, every time you swallowed your truth and called it being professional, every moment you played small instead of honoring what you actually knew.

Playing small is not just a mindset problem. It is a body problem. And your body has been sending the invoice for years.

What Cancer Taught Me About Playing Small

You already know from the last chapter that I got a cancer diagnosis and went fully into my C with it. What I didn't tell you then is what I learned while I was in it and who I became on the other side.

When I was diagnosed with breast cancer in 2024, everyone expected me to become small, grateful, and humble. Cancer patients are supposed to be quiet, compliant, thankful for whatever scraps of hope the medical establishment throws their way.

Fuck that noise.

I looked at the traditional treatment plan, looked at my own knowing, and chose to trust the one that had never steered me wrong. I went fully naturopathic and holistic, Vitamin C infusions, ozone therapy, functional medicine, and the deep unconscious reprogramming work that addressed the emotional core of what my body had been trying to say. No chemo. No radiation. My doctor thought I was out of my mind.

Five months later, I was cancer-free.

What healed alongside the physical was the part nobody talks about. Because when I got that diagnosis, I didn't just look at the tumor. I looked at what emotional tumor I had been carrying that manifested as a physical one.

I realized that for years, I had been literally suffocating my authentic self. I had been choking down my truth, swallowing my power, and apologizing for taking up space. I had been carrying the weight of everyone else's expectations while abandoning my own needs. I had been running a body that was storing decades of unresolved UDIN events, stacked on top of each other, being held in the one place I could never escape…my own cells.

The cancer wasn't happening TO me. It was my body's way of screaming: enough. Stop betraying yourself. Stop playing small. Stop apologizing for being extraordinary.

So instead of only treating the physical symptoms, I addressed the emotional and energetic core programming too. I made radical changes to everything: diet, lifestyle, mindset, environment. And most importantly, I committed to stop betraying myself. To start honoring my body's wisdom instead of overriding it. To stop playing small in the exact ways that had been costing me my health, right along with everything else.

I started speaking my truth without apology. I started saying no without a three-paragraph explanation. I started charging what I was worth without shame. I started taking up space without asking permission.

And something beautiful happened during treatment. Other patients at the holistic clinic started gravitating toward me. They'd ask when I was coming in because they wanted to be there at the same time. I'd be getting Vitamin C infusions while taking business calls about intuition and transformation, other patients would ask if they could listen. I started doing impromptu coaching sessions in the treatment room.

The old me would have said, "Oh, I'm not qualified to coach cancer patients. I'm just another patient."

The new me said, "Hell yes, let me share what I know about the power of mindset in healing."

I taught them about UDIN events. I helped them identify what emotional patterns might be contributing to their physical symptoms. I showed them how to work with their body instead of against it. The clinic staff started calling me their unofficial mindset coach. Other patients called me "the woman who beat cancer in five months."

I could have played small, kept quiet, just focused on getting through treatment.

Instead, I used my experience as a platform. Even while fighting for my life, I refused to dim my light. And I came out cancer-free. The pain of staying small eventually becomes greater than the fear of playing big. I know because I lived it in every cell of my body.

The Five Faces of Small-Playing Bullshit

Through my own journey and working with thousands of clients, I've identified the five most common ways brilliant people keep themselves in cages. Read these slowly. You may recognize yourself in more than one.

1. The Professional Apologizer This person says sorry for existing. "Sorry for the long email." "Sorry to bother you." "Sorry for taking up space." They apologize for their successes, their opinions, their needs, and their very presence on this planet. Their default setting is preemptive smallness: shrink before anyone asks you to.

2. The Credit Deflector. This person is allergic to compliments. "Oh, it was nothing." "I just got lucky." "Anyone could have done it." They bounce praise off themselves faster than a rubber ball hitting concrete. Compliments make them physically uncomfortable because receiving them would mean actually owning what they've done. And owning it means being responsible for it. And that is terrifying.

3. The Undercharging Martyr This person prices their services based on their discomfort with money rather than the value they create. They give away their expertise for free and feel guilty about charging what they're worth because "good people shouldn't care about money."

4. The Background Genius. This person has world-changing ideas but positions themselves as support staff. They're always the power behind someone else's throne, never claiming their own kingdom. They will make other people look extraordinary all day long and call it being a team player. It is not being a team player. It is being afraid to be seen.

5. The Perpetual Student This person collects certifications like Pokémon cards, always needing "just one more" before they'll consider themselves qualified to step into their power. Another course. Another credential. Another year of preparation. The learning is real. The readiness is never coming because readiness isn't the point; safety is. As long as they are still students, they cannot fail as a practitioner.

Any of these sound familiar? Most people are some combination of all five, playing small in stereo surround sound.

The Real Cost of Your Small-Playing Addiction

Playing small isn't just limiting your bigness, though that's tragic enough. Your small-playing addiction is fucking up everything around you, too.

When you play small, you teach your kids that it's dangerous to be extraordinary. You model limitations and show them that safety lies in mediocrity.

When you play small, you deprive the world of solutions it desperately needs. There are people out there who need exactly what you've got, and they can't find you because you're hiding under a bushel of false humility.

When you play small, you attract small opportunities and small people. You end up surrounded by others who need you to stay limited so they can feel better about their own small choices.

When you play small, your soul starts staging a rebellion. You know how magnificent you are, and living beneath your potential creates an internal war that manifests as anxiety, depression, frustration, and a general sense that something important is missing from your life.

When you play small, you become complicit in systems that keep brilliant people down. You participate in the collective agreement that extraordinary is too much, too threatening, too dangerous.

The cost of playing small is statistically incalculable. We'll never know what innovations didn't happen, what movements didn't start, what problems didn't get solved because someone with the solution was too busy apologizing for knowing the answer.

The Permission Slip You've Been Waiting For

I'm about to give you the permission slip you've been waiting for your entire life, so pay attention:

You are allowed to be fucking brilliant. You are allowed to charge what you're worth and then some. You are allowed to take up space, lots of it. You are allowed to have strong opinions and share them loudly. You are allowed to disagree with experts, authorities, and anyone else who thinks they know better than you do about your own life.

You are allowed to trust your instincts even when everyone else thinks you're crazy. You are allowed to be excited by your achievements without qualifying them. You are allowed to want more, much more. You are allowed to play so big that other people feel uncomfortable.

You don't need another certification, another course, another year of preparation. You don't need anyone's approval, validation, or permission except your own.

You are already qualified. You have always been enough. The only thing standing between you and the full expression of your genius is your own willingness to stop playing small.

From $7,000 to $7 Million: What Playing Big Actually Looks Like

Let me show you the difference between small-playing and big-playing with cold, hard numbers.

When I started my coaching company, I invested the initial $7,000, and it was all we had to our name. Seven thousand dollars to launch a coaching company that we hoped might someday help a few people.

For the first few years, I was still marinating in small-playing sauce:

- I introduced myself like a supporting character in my own company instead of owning my role as the visionary and strategic genius
- I undercharged because I was afraid of seeming "greedy."
- I deferred to my business partner in public even when I knew they were wrong
- I apologized for our rapid growth instead of celebrating it
- I downplayed our results instead of shouting them from the rooftops

We were successful, and we were leaving millions on the table because I was too busy playing small to claim my full power.

Then 2024 happened: cancer diagnosis plus my business partner's abrupt departure. I could either play small and close up shop or play big and step into full ownership of what we'd built.

I chose big. Unapologetically, completely, permanently big.

Instead of apologizing for the transition, I sent our entire client base an email explaining exactly what was happening and how we'd be serving them at an even higher level.

Instead of lowering prices to "make it easier" during the transition, I raised them. Instead of playing it safe, I built. A new retreat. A new certification. A new program. One after the other. While navigating the hardest year of my life.

Nine months later, the company was approaching $7 million in revenue with our highest client satisfaction rates ever. From $7,000 to $7 million in seven years. That's what happens when you stop apologizing for your genius and start leveraging it like the valuable asset it is.

Your Genius Is Non-Negotiable

Here's what you need to understand: Your genius is not optional. You can't just ignore it, suppress it, or pretend it doesn't exist.

Your genius is the unique combination of your natural gifts, your hard-earned wisdom, your distinctive perspective, and your passionate purpose. It's what you do better than anyone else on the planet. It's your irreplaceable contribution to the world.

And it's not fucking negotiable.

You can try to keep it locked up. You can apologize for it, minimize it, or hide it under layers of false humility. But it will keep pushing against whatever cage you build around it.

Your genius wants to be expressed. It wants to create value, serve people, solve problems, and make a difference. It wants to play big.

And the longer you keep it trapped in a small-playing prison, the more miserable you're going to be.

I see this with clients constantly. They come in exhausted, frustrated, feeling like something vital is missing. And when we dig deeper, we always find the same thing: massive genius being expressed at about 20% capacity.

Brilliant strategists who are stuck in jobs that require no strategic thinking. Visionary leaders playing support roles. Innovative creators who are following someone else's outdated playbook. No wonder they feel off. They are living so far below the ceiling they were built to blow through that their whole system is staging a revolt.

Here's what happens when they stop.

When they stop apologizing for their genius and start owning it, everything shifts. The right clients find them. The right opportunities line up. The income matches the value they have always been delivering. The energy comes back, real energy, clean energy, the kind that comes from finally moving in the right direction. The work lights them up. The confidence starts being something they just are. And the most common thing I hear when that happens? Why did I wait so long?

That is not a fairy tale. That is what I have watched happen, over and over: the moment someone decides that playing small is no longer an option, they are willing to choose.

You were not built for operating at 20-fucking-percent. You never were. And somewhere in your body, you have always known that.

The Playing Big Formula

Here is what it actually looks like to move from small-playing to big-fucking-playing without apology. Not a concept. Not a vibe. A concrete sequence you can use starting right now.

Step 1: Identify Your Genius Zone. What do you do that makes other people say, "Holy shit, how did you do that?" What comes so naturally to you that you assume everyone can do it? What would you do for free because you love it so much it doesn't feel like work? That intersection is your genius zone. Name it out loud. Write it down. Stop pretending you don't know what it is.

Step 2: Own Your Track Record. Stop deflecting credit and minimizing wins. Make a list of every success, every person you've helped, every positive impact you've created. Own all of it without apology. The evidence of your genius is already everywhere. You have just been trained to look away from it.

Step 3: Price Like You Mean It. Research what actual experts in your field charge, then position yourself accordingly. Your prices should reflect the value you create, not your comfort level with money. Undercharging is not generosity. It is self-betrayal with a discount code attached.

Step 4: Claim Your Fucking Space. Stop apologizing for existing. Speak up in meetings. Share your ideas with confidence. Take credit for your contributions. Ask for what you want without qualifying it to death. The space is yours. You belong in every room every single time.

Step 5: Trust Your Inner Compass. Stop deferring to external authorities when your instincts are screaming something different. You have a Four Voices framework now. You know which voice is which. Your intuition is the one that has been quietly, patiently, consistently right about you your entire life. The more you follow it, the louder it gets. The louder it gets, the easier this all becomes.

Step 6: Amplify Your Voice. Stop waiting for permission to share your message. Start speaking, writing, teaching, and creating. The world needs to hear what you have to say, so say it loudly. You are not shouting into the void. You are calling in the exact people who have been waiting for you.

The Ripple Effect of Your Bigness

When you finally stop playing small and step into your full power, something magical happens: You give everyone around you permission to do the same.

When I started owning my expertise instead of apologizing for it, my clients started owning theirs.

When I started charging premium prices for premium results, my clients started valuing themselves more highly.

When I started speaking confidently about my achievements, my clients started celebrating their wins.

When I started trusting my instincts over external authorities, my clients started trusting themselves.

Playing big isn't selfish; it's service. It's showing other people what's possible when you stop apologizing for being extraordinary.

The Time for Small Has Expired

You've been practicing small long enough. You've been apologizing long enough. You've been waiting for permission long enough.

The world is facing challenges that require extraordinary solutions. People are struggling with problems that you know how to solve. Innovations are waiting to be born that only you can create.

And none of that can happen while you're busy playing small and apologizing for your brilliance.

Playing small serves no one. It doesn't make other people feel better; it just permits them to stay limited, too. It doesn't protect you from failure; it guarantees you'll never experience the kind of success you're capable of.

Your genius is not an accident. Your gifts are not a coincidence. Your unique combination of talents, experiences, and perspectives exists for a reason.

You are here to play big. You were always meant to play big.

The only question left is: Are you ready to stop apologizing for being extraordinary and start acting like the force of nature you actually are?

Because the world is waiting for what you've got. And it's been waiting long enough.

Stop playing small. Start playing like the badass you were born to be.

The time is fucking NOW!

OWN YOUR GENIUS

You just spent an entire chapter seeing what is possible when you stop playing small and start owning your genius fully. Now we get to figure out exactly where that shift needs to happen for you specifically. Workbook out. Let's make the invisible visible and turn what you now know into something you actually live.

Week 1: The Small-Playing Audit

For the next week, become a witness to your own smallness. Every time you catch yourself doing any of the following, write it down, no judgment, just data:

- Apologizing unnecessarily
- Deflecting a compliment instead of just saying thank you
- Downplaying an achievement to make someone else comfortable
- Deferring to someone with less expertise than you
- Undercharging or giving away work for free out of guilt
- Hiding your opinion to avoid conflict
- Introducing yourself as less than you are
- Saying “I’m just” before anything

At the end of the week, look at your list. Notice the patterns. Notice which situations trigger the most smallness. Notice which of the five archetypes you are living in most of the time. That is your starting point.

Week 2: The Genius Inventory

Now flip it. This part makes people more uncomfortable than the first part, which tells you everything you need to know about how deep the small-playing programming goes. Document the evidence of your brilliance:

- Every time someone asks for your advice
- Every compliment you receive about your work
- Every problem you solve effortlessly
- Every result you create that impresses others
- Every moment when you think, "I could do this better."

Read those wins back to yourself. Out loud. Without qualifying them. Notice how uncomfortable that is. That discomfort is not humility. It is the small-playing program doing what it was installed to do.

Week 3: The Fear Excavation. Identify what you're actually afraid of:

- What specifically scares you about playing bigger?
- Whose approval would you lose if you stopped playing small?
- What responsibility would you have to accept if you owned your genius?
- What would you have to give up if you started taking up more space?

Your answers to these questions are not reasons to stay small. They are the exact places where your next level of freedom lives. Every fear you can name is a fear you can work with. Write them all down. The ones that make you squirm the most are the ones worth paying the most attention to.

Week 4: The Big-Playing Experiment. For one week, try playing bigger:

- Speak up in every meeting
- Share your opinions without apology
- Take full credit for your contributions
- Charge what you're actually worth
- Stop deflecting compliments
- Trust your instincts over others' advice

Notice what happens. Notice how people respond when you show up as the full version of yourself. Notice how your energy changes when you stop shrinking it to fit other people's comfort levels. Notice what becomes possible in just one week of deciding that your genius deserves to be seen. That is not a one-week experiment. That is the rest of your life available to you. That feeling of aliveness and rightness is not new.

It is just you, coming home to yourself. Welcome back.

CHAPTER 7
INTEGRITY:
DO WHAT YOU SAY YOU'RE GOING TO DO

"You are in integrity when the life you are living on the outside matches who you are on the inside."
— Alan Cohen

Let me tell you the thing nobody is going to tell you about confidence.

It is not a personality trait you either have or do not. It is not something you are born with or something that finally arrives one day when you have done enough work on yourself. It is not hiding in the right morning routine, the right mindset shift, or the right book. You are holding that book right now, and I am telling you straight: reading this will not give it to you.

Here is what will.

You do what you say you are going to do.

That is the whole secret. The complete answer. Every single time you follow through on a commitment you made to yourself, you deposit into the trust account you hold with the most important person in your life. Yourself.

Every time you bail on that commitment, you make a withdrawal. Do it enough times, and the account goes into overdraft. And an overdrawn self-trust account? That is what a lack of confidence actually is.

We have been out here trying to build confidence by thinking differently about ourselves. Meanwhile, the whole time it was a math problem. Deposits and withdrawals. Kept promises and broken ones. Simple, unromantic, totally unglamorous math.

Integrity is not a gold star for being a good person. It is not a personality trait. It is a practice. And it starts with the simplest, least sexy, most non-negotiable thing: doing what you said you were going to do. Not when the timing feels right. Not when you feel ready. Not after you have thought about it for six more weeks. When you fucking said you would.

The GRIT Inside InteGRITy

Look at the word. Right there in the middle of integrity, hiding in plain sight: GRIT.

Not a coincidence.

GRIT stands for Growth, Resilience, Innovation, Transformation. It is the strength of character plus the passion to keep showing up, even when showing up is inconvenient, uncomfortable, and looks nothing like the vision you had for how this was going to go.

And here is what neuroscience has to say about that combination: every single time you choose to act in alignment with your own word, even when every part of you is lobbying hard to skip it, you build a new neurological pathway. You literally rewire your brain to make showing up as the full version of yourself easier. Every time. Stacked on top of every other time.

GRIT is not about white-knuckling through pain. That is what people who have confused suffering with strength think it means. Real GRIT is about knowing exactly who you are and acting like it. Especially when it is hard. Especially when nobody is watching. Especially when bailing would be so much easier and literally nobody would blame you.

The people who build something real, real confidence, real results, real lives that they actually want to be living, are not the ones who never struggled. They are the ones who kept their word to themselves even while they were struggling.

The Promise-Breaking Habit

Be honest with me for a second.

How many times have you told yourself you were going to do something and then… didn't?

Start the business. Have the conversation. Leave the situation. Raise the prices. Take the leap. Stop the thing. Start the other thing.

And then Monday became next Monday became next month became January became maybe this isn't the right time became I'll know when I'm ready became maybe this is just who I am, someone who doesn't follow through.

I need you to hear this clearly: every single one of those broken promises is a withdrawal from your self-trust account. And your unconscious mind keeps perfect records. Meticulous, judgment-free, absolutely unforgiving records. It does not care about your reasons. It does not care that you were tired or scared or that the timing genuinely was bad. It just notes, quietly and efficiently, that when you said you would, and it got hard, you did not.

And then you wonder why confidence feels so hard to build. It is not hard to build. You just keep making withdrawals faster than you make deposits.

The good news: this is entirely fixable. It starts with the next promise you make to yourself. And whether you keep it.

The Day I Chose My Integrity Over $40,000

In 2018, a client I had been sent to save by my boss looked at me across a lunch table, told me I was absolutely incredible, and canceled her $50,000 contract.

She sent me flowers after. I am not kidding.

Her reason: "The problem is not with you or the content. The problem is with the integrity of the person running this organization. And the fact that he sent you to clean up his mess instead of taking responsibility himself tells me everything I need to know."

I sat with that the entire drive home.

She was right. I had been watching it for months. Promises made to clients that quietly evaporated. Commitments that got creatively reframed when honoring them became inconvenient. And I had been rationalizing it, accommodating it, telling myself it was not that bad, that this was just how business worked, that I could make it work from the inside.

What I was actually doing was allowing someone else's lack of integrity to erode mine. Slowly. Incrementally. In ways I barely noticed until a woman I had never met handed me a mirror over a Caesar salad and changed everything.

I left. I walked away from $40,000 in back pay, a stable paycheck, and a role I was genuinely excellent at. My assistant Alex quit the same day without even needing a conversation about it.

Here is what I know now. You cannot stay in an environment that operates without integrity and keep yours intact. It is not a willpower problem. It is not a strength problem. It is not possible because integrity is contagious in both directions. You become what you tolerate. And I was done tolerating that.

The hard part was never leaving. The hard part was seeing it clearly enough to go.

When Keeping Your Word Costs Everything

The month before I officially beat cancer, my business partner left our company.

Without warning. Without a plan. And in a way that left me holding every single client commitment, every program promise, every relationship we had built, entirely by myself.

Let me paint you a picture of what that actually looked like. I was knee deep in my cancer treatments, seeing the light at the end of the tunnel. I had just fought for my life for the last 4 months, done the deep reprogramming work, emerged on the other side, and was rebuilding my health with everything I had. And now I was also rebuilding my entire business alone.

Nobody would have blamed me for closing the doors. Not one person in my life would have called it quitting. I had a better excuse than most people will ever have. I could have walked away completely clean.

I honored every single client agreement instead.

Every. Single. Fucking. One. Not one person lost the program they had paid for. Not one promise got quietly revised because it had become inconvenient. Not one client was left holding the cost of something that had nothing to do with them. I carried the full weight of every commitment we had made, and I delivered on all of it.

Not because it was easy. Because my word meant something. Because integrity is not a fair-weather practice. It is the thing you do precisely when you have every justification in the world not to. That is when it counts. That is when it builds something.

That decision became the foundation for everything that came next.

What InteGRITy Actually Builds

Let me show you what a life built on inteGRITy actually produces. Not as a concept. As a result.

My company reached its first million dollars in revenue entirely through referrals in the first 2 years, one of which was during a global pandemic (no biggie). No advertising budget. No paid campaigns. People who experienced the work told other people about it because it delivered exactly what it promised. We maintain an over an 80% client rollover rate year after year. You do not get numbers like that through a clever marketing strategy. You get them by doing what you said you would do, every time, for years, until trust becomes your reputation.

I hold the Presidential Lifetime Achievement Award for my service and dedication to helping others transform their lives. I am one of only 150 Internationally Accredited NLP Master Trainers in the entire world. And on top of all of that, I was nominated and accepted into the Royal Order of the Principality of Cappadocia, an extremely distinguished honor, recognizing excellence in science, business, philanthropy, and character. I was nominated and accepted under 'Entrepreneurship and Innovation'.

I did not receive those things because I was the loudest or the most aggressive or the best at promoting myself. I received them because of what I built and how I built it. Over decades. Through infertility, divorce, foreclosure, betrayal, a class action lawsuit, cancer, and a business partner walking out as I was at the finish line of beating cancer.

None of it without inteGRITy at the center.

This is not a brag. This is evidence. This is what it looks like when you decide your word means something and you refuse to compromise it regardless of the cost. The world notices. The right people notice. And what gets built on that foundation is something that lasts.

How to Rebuild InteGRITy With Yourself

If you have been breaking promises to yourself long enough that you have stopped noticing, here is what you do NOT do. You do not make a dramatic recommitment to ten huge things and try to overhaul your entire life by next Tuesday. That is just the A-B cycle in a new outfit. It feels productive for about four days, and then you are right back where you started, except now you have more evidence against yourself.

Here is what you actually do.

You make one promise. One. Small enough to keep. Specific enough to know whether you kept it. And then you keep it.

Not because it is going to change your life overnight. Simply because you said you would. And that matters. Because the next time you make a promise to yourself, you will have one data point that says: I showed up for me. And the time after that, two. And the time after that, three. And at some point, that account has enough in it that you start to feel it. The quiet, solid, unshakeable confidence of someone who knows that when she says she is going to do something, she does it.

That is not a personality trait. That is a track record you built on purpose.

Growth. Resilience. Innovation. Transformation. Built one kept promise at a time. That is inteGRITy. And it changes everything from the inside out.

The Bridge: From InteGRITy to Wealth

Once you are living in integrity with yourself, keeping your word, showing up for yourself the way you have always shown up for everyone else, something starts to shift in the way you see money.

Because here is what I know to be true after building a seven-figure company from a $7,000 starting point through more adversity than most people face in a lifetime: you cannot build sustainable wealth on a foundation of broken promises and suppressed inner knowing. You can make money that way. Plenty of people do. But it will always feel like it could disappear. Because it is not built on something real.

Real wealth, the kind that gives you actual freedom and actual choices and the ability to live on your own actual terms, starts with exactly what we have been building in this chapter. It starts with trusting yourself. It starts with knowing your worth. It starts with refusing to accept less than what you know to be true, from yourself first and from everyone else second.

Once you have that foundation, you are ready to talk about money.

And that is exactly what comes next.

YOUR INTEGRITY INVENTORY

You just spent an entire chapter learning that confidence is not something you find. It is built, one kept promise at a time. Now we are going to figure out exactly where yours has been leaking and plug the hole. No theory. No inspiration. Just you, a pen, your workbook, and the honest answers you have been dancing around. The places that make you want to skip ahead? Those are exactly the places to slow down.

PART 1: YOUR PROMISE AUDIT

What have you been telling yourself you were going to do and not doing? Write it all down. The business thing. The health thing. The conversation you keep postponing. The decision you keep almost making. All of it. Get it out of your head and onto the page where you can actually see it.

- What I have been telling myself I would do:
- How long have I been telling myself this:
- The story I keep telling myself about why I haven't:
- What this broken promise has actually been costing me in confidence and self-trust:

PART 2: THE ENVIRONMENT CHECK

Is there any area in your life right now where you are tolerating an environment that is operating out of integrity? A relationship, a job, a situation where someone else's lack of integrity is quietly becoming the water you swim in? Because you cannot stay in that water and keep yourself clean.

- Where am I tolerating something I know is out of alignment?
- What is staying there actually costing me?
- What would choosing my integrity over my comfort look like here?

PART 3: YOUR INTEGRITY WINS

This is the part people skip. Do not skip it. Your brain is wired to catalog the failures and gloss over the evidence that you are actually already showing up for yourself. We are fixing that right now.

- Three times in the last month, I kept a promise to myself:
- What does that tell me about who I already am?

PART 4: THE ONE PROMISE

Not ten. One. The promise that matters most right now. The one you have been pushing off. The one that, if you kept it, would change how you feel about yourself more than anything else on the list. Pick it. Write it down. Commit to it.

- The one promise I am making to myself right now:
- Exactly how I am going to keep it, starting today:
- What is going to be built in me by keeping this promise:

Now write this. By hand. Slowly. Mean every single word.

"I am someone who keeps their word. Especially to myself. Especially when it is hard. Especially when no one is watching. Starting now."

Read it out loud. Let it land somewhere real.

That is not a journal prompt. That is a decision about who you are.

The version of you that keeps her promises is not a future version you are working toward. She is the version that shows up today, does the thing she said she would do, and deposits one more piece of evidence into the account that says: I can trust myself.

Build that account. One day at a time. One kept promise at a time.

That is inteGRITy. And it changes everything.

CHAPTER 8
The Wealth Code:
Stop Apologizing for Wanting Money and Start Creating It

"If you want to find the secrets of the universe, think in terms of energy, frequency, and vibration"
— Nikola Tesla

Let's get something straight right now.

Money is not the root of all evil. It is not a necessary inconvenience. It is not a dirty word or a spiritual compromise or something you are supposed to want only a little of while pretending you are fine with whatever shows up. Money is a positive exchange of energy. And like all energy, it responds to frequency and vibration. Which means the way you think about it, feel about it, and show up in relationship to it is not just a mindset issue. It is a vibrational one.

Here is the definition I want you to burn into your brain and never let go of.

Wealth is money at a high vibration.

Read that again. Wealth is not a number. It is not a milestone. It is not something you eventually arrive at when you have done enough, worked enough, or earned the right to stop apologizing for wanting it. Wealth is a state of being. A frequency. An energetic relationship with money that you either hold or do not. And right now, most people are trying to build wealth while vibrating at the exact frequency that repels it.

That ends here.

Everything Is Energy. Including Your Bank Account.

Nikola Tesla said it, and quantum physics has spent the last century proving it: everything in existence is energy, everything has a frequency, and everything has a vibration. The chair you are sitting in. The air you are breathing. The thoughts running through your head right now. The number in your bank account. All of it is energy expressing itself at a particular frequency.

This is not woo. This is physics.

And here is what it means for your money. The wealth you want already exists. It is not hiding from you. It is not being withheld from you as punishment for your limiting beliefs, your difficult childhood, or the years you spent playing small. It is simply vibrating at a different frequency than the one you are currently at. And energy, by its nature, wants to match the vibration around it.

So the question is not whether wealth is available to you. Of course it is. The universe is not operating from scarcity. There is not a finite supply of abundance that runs out before it gets to you. The universe is constantly expanding because we as a human race are constantly expanding, and there is no ceiling on that growth.

The question is whether what you want vibrates where you are.

That is the whole game. And once you understand it, everything changes.

The Vibration Scale and Why Desire Is Not Your Friend

Here is one of the most important things I have learned in decades of doing this work.

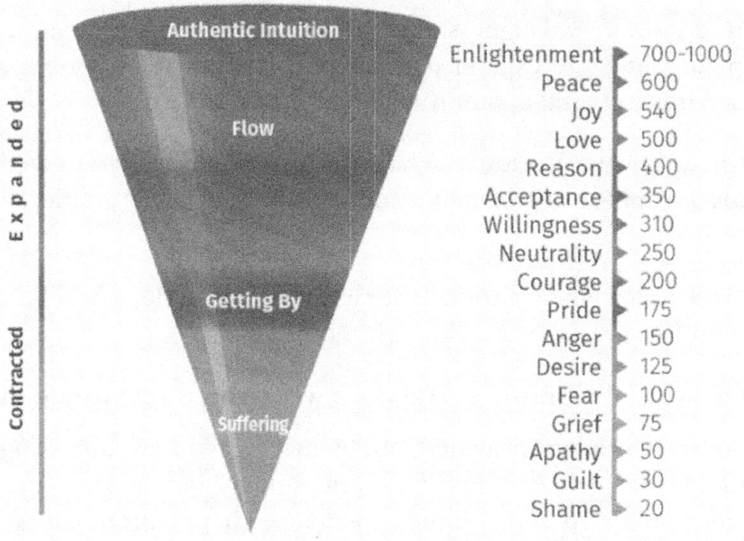

Desire presupposes lack.

Abraham Hicks will tell you that desire is where creation begins, and they are absolutely right. Contrast happens, you experience what you do not want, desire is born, the rocket launches. That part is working.

The problem is what happens next, which for most people is absolutely nothing. They launch the rocket, and then they just stand there staring at the sky, camping in the wanting, running on the hustle and grind, and sweaty desperation of not having it yet.

And here is the thing about that. Desire sits at 125 on the vibration scale. Contracted energy. Just above Fear. Nowhere near the expanded states where wealth is actually hanging out. The universe is not responding to your goals. It is not responding to your vision board or your five-year plan or the really compelling speech you gave yourself in the bathroom mirror this morning.

It is responding to your dominant vibration. And if that vibration is wanting, it will keep delivering more wanting back to you with impeccable accuracy and absolutely zero judgment.

The work is not to work harder. It is to move up the scale.

From desire to willingness. From willingness to acceptance. From acceptance into the expanded frequency of someone who has already decided it is hers and is simply waiting for the delivery.

That is where the Vortex is. That is where everything you asked for is already assembled and waiting. Launch the rocket. Then go meet it at the top.

This is the Hawkins emotional vibration scale in action. And here is the question I want you to sit with right now.

Where are you vibrating? And does what you want vibrate there?

If you are vibrating in anxiety about money, you are attracting more situations that generate anxiety about money. If you are vibrating in scarcity, you are attracting more experiences that confirm scarcity. Your vibration is your set point, and the universe is endlessly, efficiently, non-judgmentally delivering experiences that match it. It is not punishing you. It is just doing what energy does.

The work is not to want more. The work is to become the frequency of what you want.

The Lies You've Been Fed

Before we get into how wealth actually works, we need to clear out some seriously fucked up programming. Most people are walking around with poverty consciousness dressed up as virtue. Let's burn it down.

Lie #1: Money doesn't buy happiness.

Tell that to the person who cannot pay rent. Money does not buy fulfillment; that is true. And it is a whole lot easier to find fulfillment when you are not in survival mode. And making decisions from survival mode is not a vibration; it is a prison.

Lie #2: Money is the root of all evil.

Money is neutral. It amplifies who you already are. Generous? More money makes you more generous. An asshole? More money makes you a bigger asshole. The money itself is completely innocent. Stop blaming the tool for what humans do with it.

Lie #3: You can't be spiritual and wealthy.

Says who? Some of the most spiritually evolved people I know are also some of the wealthiest. They use their resources to serve, fund meaningful work, and create real change in the world. Poverty is not a virtue. It is just fucking poverty.

Lie #4: Rich people are greedy and selfish.

Some are. So are some broke people. Greed is not income-dependent. Generosity is not income-dependent either. Some of the most generous humans I have ever met have a lot of money, and they give it freely. Stop using other people's bad behavior as a reason to stay small.

Lie #5: Be grateful for what you have and stop wanting more.

Gratitude and ambition are not enemies. You can be deeply grateful AND be working to create more. Wanting more does not make you ungrateful. It makes you someone who knows they have more to give if they had more to give.

These lies were installed before you had any say in the matter. And they have been quietly running the show ever since. It is time to update this software.

The Unconscious Programs Running Your Financial Life

Your conscious mind is the goal setter. Your unconscious mind is the goal getter. A short recap from Chapter 3: The conscious mind is about five percent of your total mental processing. The unconscious mind is the other ninety-five. It runs every automatic behavior, every habitual pattern, every emotionally charged belief you have ever absorbed, at approximately 500,000 times the processing speed of your conscious mind.

So when your conscious mind says I want to make $100,000 this year and your unconscious mind is running a program that says people like me do not make that kind of money, or if I get rich, people will not like me, guess who wins? The unconscious. Every single time.

Here are the programs most likely running in your background right now if you aren't hitting the goals you are setting.

The Scarcity Program.

"There is not enough to go around." It has you hoarding, competing, and making every financial decision from fear instead of possibility. Exhausting. Expensive. And not true.

The Unworthiness Program.

"People like me do not get to have wealth." The sneaky one. It will have you unconsciously passing up opportunities, undervaluing your work, and somehow always ending up with just slightly less than enough. It is not bad luck. It is a god-damn program.

The Guilt Program.

"It is selfish to want money." It makes you feel vaguely terrible every time you charge what you are actually worth. So you do not. And then you resent or judge everyone who does.

The Safety Program.

It is safer to be poor than rich. Wealth brings visibility, judgment, and responsibility. And your unconscious mind, whose number one job is keeping you safe, has decided that staying small is the safer bet. It is wrong, and very convincing.

The Identity Program.

"I am just not a money person." When wealth feels foreign to your identity, your unconscious mind will reject it the same way your body rejects an organ that does not match. You cannot create what you cannot conceive of as yours.

Until these programs get cleared and replaced with something that actually serves you, your conscious mind can set financial goals all day long. Your unconscious will quietly, efficiently, sabotage every single one. Not because it is against you. Because it is trying to protect an identity that no longer serves you.

The WEALTH Framework: What It Actually Takes

Over years of working with thousands of people on their relationship with money, I distilled it down to six elements in an easy-to-remember acronym.

W — Willing.

You have to be willing. Willing to look at your money story honestly. Willing to move from effect to cause. Willing to let go of the beliefs, emotions, and behaviors that have been running the show up until now. Some of you are willing to look at almost everything, and then you hit the one thing, and you go, "I will do anything but that." And here's what I know: that one thing is exactly where everything you want is waiting. The unwillingness is the wall. And everything you are after is on the other side of it.

E — Empower.

You deserve to be empowered from the inside out. And that starts with understanding that money is not just a financial tool; it is life. Without it, you cannot live, cannot shelter yourself, cannot eat, cannot show up for the people you love, cannot build the impact you came here to make. You were not put on this earth for survival. Animals survive. Humans are built for so much more. You were brought into this world as a winner. You beat astronomical odds to be here. Stop accepting a survival existence as your ceiling.

A — Awareness.

You need to know where your money is going and what it is doing. Not from anxiety or obsession, but from the empowered awareness of someone who is in relationship with their finances rather than running from them. A rocket is off course ninety-seven percent of the time on its way to the moon. Ninety-seven percent. And it still gets there because it stays focused on the destination and makes constant small course corrections. You can be off course most of the time and still arrive exactly where you are going. The key is knowing where you are so you can redirect toward where you want to be.

L — Leverage.

Working harder is not the answer. The hardest working person in any room is seldom the wealthiest. If effort alone created wealth, every laborer would be a millionaire. Wealth is created through leverage. Leveraging your unconscious mind. Leveraging financial systems. Leveraging the right tools that multiply your time, your energy, and your money instead of just depleting them. We call one of these tools "*Purple Magic Money™*," and we will get to it shortly because it is one of the most powerful manifestation practices we have.

T — Towards.

Your motivation has to be towards what you want, not away from what you do not want. Away-from motivation is exhausting because the moment you put enough distance between yourself and the thing you are fleeing, the motivation disappears, and you snap back and start all over. Towards motivation is self-sustaining because the goal itself generates the energy. When you find yourself thinking I do not want to be broke or I do not want to be stressed about money…STOP. Ask yourself: what do I want instead? Write it down. Say it out loud. Make it specific. That redirection is not a small thing. It is a complete reprogramming of the direction your unconscious mind is pointed.

H — Holistic.

Your relationship with money is not a financial issue in isolation. It is connected to your identity, your emotional history, your physical body, your spiritual connection, and every other area of your life. The core program of your money challenges might be living in a completely different area of your life. You cannot solve it by addressing the symptom. You have to find the core. And when you work holistically, when you do the work on the mental, emotional, physical, and spiritual bodies, everything shifts. Not just your bank account. Your whole life.

Purple Magic Money™: Manifestation Made Real

Let me tell you about one of the most powerful practices we use within my company, and I am going to let the moment it was born tell you everything you need to know. A client was sitting with her wealth tracker, watching what was happening in real time, and she was stunned. Speechless. And then not speechless at all because she could not stop saying *this is magic, this is actual magic.* She looked at the purple-highlighted numbers glowing back at her from the screen, and the name came out of nowhere and everywhere at once: ***Purple Magic Money™***. She could not think of any other way to describe it. Honestly? Neither could we.

Inside our wealth tracker, everything is color-coded: your income, your expenses, your projections, your debt payoff. And then there is the purple-highlighted line. That line tracks something most people never think to measure: the money that finds *you.* The credit card rewards. The surprise refund. The discount you never asked for. The bill that disappeared. The income is already moving in your direction because your vibration called it in before your bank account knew it was coming.

Free money. Surprise money. Money you did not have to grind for, hustle for, or chase. Money that most people walk right past without ever recognizing it for what it is, proof that abundance is already moving in their direction.

Here is what Purple Magic Money™ looks like in real life:

You were fully prepared to pay full price for something, and at the last moment, you discover there is a discount or a bonus you did not know existed. That difference? Purple Magic Money™.

Your credit card rewards accumulate, and suddenly you have hundreds of dollars available that required nothing extra from you. Purple Magic Money™.

You find a twenty-dollar bill in a jacket pocket, a gift card you forgot about, and cash in an old purse. Purple Magic Money™.

You planned to pay for something, and it gets covered, a friend insists on treating you, a company sends a refund you forgot you were owed, or a deal falls through in your favor. Purple Magic Money™.

You braced yourself for a major expense, let's say a new roof; you had every intention of paying for it, you had mentally released the money, and then at the last minute, your insurance company covered it in full. That entire amount lives in your Purple Magic Money™ column. Unexpected upgrades. Windfalls. Gifts. A bill that simply disappears. All of it counts.

What makes Purple Magic Money™ so powerful is not just what it is, but what it does to you when you receive it.

When you recognize Purple Magic Money™ and celebrate it, your vibration rises. And when your vibration rises, you become a match for even more. This is why Purple Magic Money™ is not just a feel-good concept; it is an **accelerator of manifestation**.

The moment you acknowledge it, honor it, and feel genuine gratitude for it, you activate a cycle. More flows in because you are now operating from the frequency of someone who receives.

The problem is that most people do not celebrate it. Most people do not even notice it. The discount registers as luck. The refund gets lost in the noise of a busy week. The insurance payout gets filed away as a relief rather than recognized as evidence of a working, breathing abundance practice. And because it never lands in their conscious awareness, it never compounds.

This is why we track it.

When you bring Purple Magic Money™ into your conscious awareness, when you write it down, add it to your tracker, and watch the number grow, something shifts every time. You start *looking* for it. You start *expecting* it. You move from a mindset of scarcity and effort into an abundance mindset where passive money is not a fantasy; it is a pattern you are actively building. You begin to see that money does not only come from hard work. It comes from alignment. It comes from frequency. It comes from who you are becoming. It can and will come easily and effortlessly.

And here is the magic of tracking it over time: the number accumulates. Every gift card, every reward, every unexpected upgrade, every bill that vanished, they add up. When clients see their Purple Magic Money™ total for the first time, many are stunned. Thousands of dollars they had unconsciously received and never fully claimed. Once they see it, they cannot unsee it. And once you cannot unsee abundance, you stop living inside the story that money is hard to come by.

Purple Magic Money™ also invites you to start thinking more strategically. Which credit cards are you using that could be generating the highest rewards? Are you enrolling in loyalty programs? Are you paying attention to what is available to you that you have been leaving on the table? This is not about obsessing over pennies; it is about training your mind and your systems to be *receptive* to abundance in every form it chooses to arrive.

Celebrate every single dollar of it. Not because the amount is always large, because celebration is the energetic signal that says: *I am someone who receives. I am someone who notices. I am someone who expects more.* And the universe, your unconscious mind, your entire energetic field, it responds to that signal every time.

One of my clients, named Claire, had been in what she described as a very dry year and a half in her business. She was doing all the right things. She was showing up. She was working. And nothing was moving. Then she went through the wealth work with us, cleared her unconscious core programs, raised her vibration, and added the purple magic money™ line to her tracker.

Within two weeks, her husband had booked two new clients, and she had not one but two large contracts land in her lap. Both within the same window. And if that was not enough, they received word that their brand-new rental property had just gone into a three-year contract, which meant their mortgage was covered and they were immediately cash flow positive on a property they had just acquired. Not eventually. Not someday. Day one. She got on our group call and said, I cannot explain this other than Purple Magic Money™.

She was not wrong.

What Claire experienced was not luck. It was vibrational alignment. She had done the internal work, shifted her frequency, and made a tangible, daily practice of holding the energy of what she was calling in. The purple magic money line on her tracker was not just a number. It was an act of conscious manifestation. A declaration to her unconscious mind and to the universe that she was operating from a different set point now.

Because here is what I know to be true about manifestation: it is not passive. You do not write something down once and then sit back and wait. Manifestation is the active practice of becoming the frequency of what you want. Of clearing everything in your unconscious that contradicts it. Of taking inspired action from that aligned state instead of throwing effort at the wall and hoping something sticks.

Inspired action and regular action are not the same thing. Regular action is like throwing wet paper towels against a wall. Someone can walk by and sweep all of it away in one move. Inspired action is like drilling a molly screw into the wall and hanging your dreams on it. It does not fall off. Because it is anchored in something real. It comes from inside you, from alignment, from the version of you who has already decided that what you want is not just possible but inevitable.

That is what the Purple Magic Money™ line represents. That is what manifestation actually is.

From $7,000 to $7 Million

I want to tell you about a woman who started a coaching company with $7,000 and no safety net. No investors. No guarantee of anything. Just a deep, absolute knowing that she was supposed to do this work in the world, and a commitment to staying in the frequency of that knowing, no matter what life threw at her.

That woman is me.

When we launched Genius Unlocked, the circumstances were not favorable by any external measure. I was starting fresh. I had cleared out the old, done the deep unconscious work on my own money story, and I had made a decision that I was going to operate from a completely different vibration than the one I had been living in. Not from fear of failure. Not from desperation. From the frequency of someone who knows her work changes lives and is willing to show up that way completely, without apology, without hedging, without playing small to make other people comfortable.

I did not reach $7 million because I worked harder than everyone else. I reached it because I got into alignment. Because I cleared the programs that had been quietly running interference on every financial goal I had set for years. Because I stopped vibrating in scarcity and started vibrating in the frequency of someone who creates wealth and has always been meant to.

The first million came entirely through referrals. No advertising. No complex funnels. People who had experienced the transformation told other people about it because it had delivered exactly what it promised. That is not a marketing strategy. That is what happens when you are operating in full alignment. When your vibration and your work and your identity are all pointing in the same direction, the universe stops working against you and starts working with you.

From $7,000 to $7 million. That is not a hustle story. That is a frequency story.

What Wealth Actually Provides: The Cancer Lesson

When I was diagnosed with breast cancer, one of the things that became immediately clear, alongside everything else you feel in that moment, was how differently I was able to meet that diagnosis because of the wealth I had built.

The holistic treatment protocol I chose was entirely out of pocket. High-dose Vitamin C infusions, ozone therapy, naturopathic, and functional medicine. Five months of intensive treatment. Over $80,000 in cash and 0% credit cards (#purplemagicmoney™).

The ability to buy my own equipment so that I can maintain my health for years to come was a way to leverage the wealth I had built. Over $50,000 in equipment that I not only get to use myself, but I get to share the wealth with my girls and my friends.

Ten years earlier, that would have been impossible. I would have been forced to choose treatment based on what insurance covered rather than what I believed would actually heal my body.

I would have been deciding my own life, the most intimate possible decision, from scarcity rather than from a woman who finally knew her worth.

The wealth I had built meant I did not have to do that. I made that decision based on my values and my knowing, not my limitations. And I came out cancer-free.

That is what wealth actually provides. Not stuff. Not status. Not the ability to flex. It gives choices. Freedom. The ability to move through your life, through the hardest moments of your life, according to what actually matters most to you. The ability to say this is what I believe is right for my body, and I have the resources to honor that.

If that is not leverage in action, I don't know what is.

How to Raise Your Vibration and Create Wealth on Purpose

This is the part where we get practical. Because all the vibration talk in the world does not create results without the actual work of shifting your frequency. And that work is both internal and external.

Step 1: Get fucking honest about where you are vibrating.

Not where you want to be. Not where you perform being. Where you actually are. When you think about money, what emotions come up? Fear? Anxiety? Shame? Resentment? Those are vibrational signatures. Write them down. See them clearly. You cannot change what you will not look at directly.

Step 2: Clear the core programming that is keeping you at that frequency.

This is not positive thinking, your way past old beliefs. This is releasing them at the unconscious level where they actually live, permanently. NLP, Quantum Release, breathwork, somatic release, energy work, hypnotherapy. The tools that get underneath the surface and actually clear what is running. Because you cannot logic your way out of an unconscious program. You have to go where it lives.

Step 3: Install the new frequency.

You do not just clear the old. You install the new. You consciously decide what vibration you are choosing to operate from. Not "I am trying to become wealthy". It becomes "I am someone who creates wealth. Not someday. Now". That is a different identity. A different frequency. A different set of instructions to your unconscious mind.

Step 4: Take inspired action from that frequency.

Raise your prices. Charge based on transformation, not time or fear. Make financial decisions from alignment instead of desperation. Every action you take from your new frequency reinforces the new program and starves the old one. Every time you show up as the version of you who creates wealth, you are voting for that version to be real.

Step 5: Hold the purple line.

Keep a daily practice of consciously holding the energy of what you are calling in. Know what it is. Write it down. Feel it as already real. Not as wishful thinking but as vibrational certainty. This is a manifestation as a practice, not an event. This is what separates the people who get results from the people who get interesting journal entries. Embrace your Purple Magic Money™.

Stop Apologizing for Abundance

You are allowed to want money. You are allowed to create wealth. You are allowed to reprogram your unconscious mind so that it supports your financial goals instead of quietly dismantling every single one of them.

You are allowed to charge what you are worth. To want more than just enough. To enjoy beautiful things without drowning in guilt. To be both deeply spiritual and seriously wealthy. To use money as the tool it actually is. A tool for freedom. A tool for impact. A tool for creating the kind of life where you get to make your decisions based on your values instead of your limitations.

Your wealth is not separate from your purpose. It is the resource that fuels it. Every dollar you create and keep and grow is an amplification of everything you are here to do. You cannot serve at your highest level from a place of financial stress. You cannot create the impact you came here to make while running in survival mode. Wealth is not the opposite of integrity, spirituality, or depth. It is the thing that lets all of those things operate at full capacity.

Your wealthy self is not some distant future version of you that you have to earn your way into. She is the version of you that exists when you finally stop arguing for your limitations. When you stop apologizing for what you want. When you step all the way into the frequency of someone who creates wealth and refuses to apologize for it.

She has always been there. You were just too busy playing small to let her in.

YOUR WEALTH CODE ACTIVATION

You just spent an entire chapter learning that wealth is not just a financial strategy; it is a frequency. And now we are going to get specific about where your frequency is set, what is keeping it there, and what you are going to do to shift it. Three practices. All three matter. Don't just pick your favorite and skip the others.

PRACTICE 1: YOUR VIBRATION AUDIT

Before you can shift your frequency, you have to know where it is. Not where you want it to be. Where it actually is right now. Answer these honestly. No Bull Shit. No performance. No curated self-awareness. The real answer.

- When I think about money, the emotions that come up most consistently are:
- The money story I absorbed before age ten is still running:
- The sentence I would finish if I said "When it comes to money, people like me…":
- The vibration I am currently operating from when it comes to wealth (circle the most honest one): Remember no bullshit

Apathy Fear Desire / Wanting Anger
Willingness Acceptance Abundance

- What this vibration has been costing me in real terms.
- The one unconscious program most likely running the show in my financial life right now.

PRACTICE 2: BUILD YOUR CASH BOX

When was the last time you actually held a meaningful amount of cash in your hands? Not swiped a card. Not moved a number on a screen. Actually held it, counted it, felt the weight of it in your hands.

For most people, the answer is never or a very long time ago. And that matters more than you think. Your unconscious mind learns through experience and sensation, not logic. If money has always felt scarce, stressful, or just abstract, your nervous system is going to keep treating it that way, no matter how many affirmations you read.

The cash box changes that. Here is how.

Get a box.

Beautiful or basic, a decorative box, a wooden keepsake box, something that feels special and intentional. This is your wealth container. Treat it like one.

Fill it with cash.

Go get 100 one-dollar bills. Pull out whatever is in your wallet. Add what you can. The amount matters less than the practice. The goal is a physical, tangible representation of wealth that you can see, touch, and count.

Count it every day.

Every morning or evening, open the box and count the money out loud, slowly, all the way to 100. While you count, you are not thinking about what it cannot buy or how it is not enough. You are thinking: I am someone who has money. Money flows to me. There is always more coming.

Add to it when money comes in.

Every time you receive money, a payment, a refund, or a gift, put some in the box first. Before the bills, before the expenses. Let your unconscious mind experience what it feels like to accumulate rather than immediately deplete.

Your unconscious mind does not know the difference between $500 in a box and $500,000 in an account. What it knows is how it feels to be in the presence of money. Train it to feel good. Train it to feel like home.

Wealth Tip: Add a Citrine stone to your cash box because it will attract wealth, prosperity, and financial abundance!

PRACTICE 3: ACTIVATE YOUR PURPLE MAGIC MONEY™

This is your manifestation practice. Not wishful thinking. Not a vision board you look at once. The active, intentional, daily practice of holding the frequency of what you are calling in.

Starting today, you are going to track every dollar of Purple Magic Money™ that comes your way. Here is how:

Step 1: Open a new column, a new note, a new page, whatever works for you, and title it Purple Magic Money™. This is your dedicated space for every dollar that finds you without force.

Step 2: Go back and populate it. Think about the last 30, 60, 90 days. What discounts landed in your lap? What rewards accumulated quietly? What bill went away? What showed up unexpectedly? Write it down and add it up. You may be stunned by what is already there.

Step 3: Every time Purple Magic Money™ arrives, log it immediately and celebrate it out loud. Not in your head. Out loud. Say thank you. Do a little dance. Text a friend. The celebration is not optional; it is the mechanism. It is what signals to your nervous system, your unconscious mind, and your energetic field that you are someone who receives.

Step 4: Watch the number grow. Do not just track it and forget it. Come back to it. Let the accumulating total be evidence that abundance is not something you are waiting for; it is something that is already happening.

Here is what this chapter has been asking you to do the whole time: see money differently.

Not as something you chase, stress over, or secretly feel you do not deserve. But as energy. As frequency. As something that responds to *you*! To your willingness, your awareness, your leverage, your forward focus, and your commitment to living in full integrity with what you say you want.

The WEALTH framework is not a formula. It is a way of being. And when you operate from that place…when you are **W**illing to rewire, **E**mpowered by a new definition of wealth, **A**ware of where your money is and where it is going, **L**everaging every tool available to you, moving **T**owards what you want instead of away from what you fear, and living **H**olistically as a person whose inner and outer worlds are in alignment, money stops being the problem. It becomes the proof.

Add Purple Magic Money™ to that equation, and you have something even more powerful. You have evidence. Real, trackable, accumulating evidence that abundance is not a someday thing. It is a right now thing. It is the discount, the reward, the refund, the bill that disappeared, the roof your insurance company paid for. It is the universe meeting you at your vibration and saying *yes.*

Start tracking it. Start celebrating it. Start expecting it.

Because the moment you stop waiting for wealth to arrive and start recognizing that it is already here, that is when everything accelerates.

CHAPTER 9
THE RIPPLE EFFECT:
HOW YOUR TRANSFORMATION CHANGES EVERYTHING

"Thousands of candles can be lit from a single candle, and the life of the candle will not be shortened. Happiness never decreases by being shared."
— Buddha

Your transformation is not just about you. It never was.

Most personal development books will not say this because it sounds too big, and they are scared you won't believe it. So I am going to say it anyway: the work you just did does not stay inside you. It leaks. Gloriously, uncontrollably, beautifully leaks into every person, every room, every conversation you walk into.

You have already changed people you have not even met yet. The second you start operating from your actual genius, people feel it before you say a single word about it. Not because you explained your transformation. Because you ARE your transformation now. That is not a responsibility to manage carefully. That is the most natural, unstoppable, electric thing about where you are standing right now. You'd better own it!

This is how energy works.

There is a concept in physics and in energy work called entrainment. It is the phenomenon where two energy systems in proximity begin to synchronize. The classic example is pendulum clocks on a shared wall eventually swinging in unison. Your heartbeat synchronizes with music. Your nervous system settles when you are near someone calm.

Or, in the version that is less fun to reckon with, your energy contracts when you spend extended time around people vibrating in fear, scarcity, and smallness. Entrainment does not ask permission. It just happens.

What this means for you is profound. When you raise your vibration, when you do the real work that shifts your frequency from contracted to expanded, from survival to flow, you do not just change your own experience of the world. You change the energetic field you carry into every room, every relationship, every conversation. You become a different force in the lives of the people around you. Not because you said anything different. Because you are different. And energy, as we established in the last chapter, always wants to match the vibration around it.

You are about to become someone's spark.

You may already be. You probably already are, and you just have not fully seen the reach of it yet.

And one more thing before we move on, because this comes up and it deserves a direct answer. Yes, your transformation will affect your relationships. No, that is not something to be afraid of. The people whose connection with you deepens as you grow are showing you who your people actually are.

The relationships that feel more strained as you step into your full self are showing you something important, too, about where the connection was built and whether it has the capacity to hold who you are becoming.

People come into our lives for a reason, a season, or a lifetime.

The work is not to hold every relationship in the lifetime category, regardless of what it actually is. The work is to be honest about which one it is, to bring your full self to the ones that can hold it, and to release the ones that are complete with the same grace you would offer anything that served you well. Your growth is not the problem. And the relationships that make it through that growth are the ones worth everything.

The Day My Daughter Quit College

Let me tell you about the phone call that made me realize my daughter had been paying attention to a lot more than I thought.

Isabella went to college excited. She had grown up inside this work, watched transformation happen in real time, lived with the neuroscience and the frameworks and the results all around her, and she wanted to go deeper. She wanted to understand the science behind why it worked. Psychology seemed like the obvious path.

Halfway through her second semester, she called me, and I could already tell from her tone that something had shifted. She had realized that every single one of her psychology classes was teaching the same material over and over again, just through different lenses and different textbooks. So she did what I have watched her do her whole life when something stops making sense: she pivoted.

She switched to education. If the formal systems were not teaching people how to actually understand themselves and each other, maybe the answer was to get into those systems early and change what was being taught.

Then her education department head handed back a final essay with feedback that stopped her cold.

Isabella had written about emotional intelligence and its potential to address bullying in schools. The kind of deeply researched, practically grounded work that comes from someone who has not just read about emotional intelligence but watched it change people's lives from the inside out. The department head's response?

"I don't understand how emotional intelligence might stop or change bullying."

Read that again.

The person responsible for training the next generation of educators did not understand how emotional intelligence might change bullying.

Isabella sat with that feedback and realized she was not looking at a gap in her own knowledge. She was looking at a gap in the institution's knowledge. She had seen people clear decades of pain in months through this work. She had watched programs that therapists said would take years of treatment dissolve in days.

She had grown up surrounded by the evidence of what becomes possible when you actually work at the level where behavior lives. And she was sitting in classrooms being taught by people who were still asking whether emotional intelligence was relevant.

She called me and told me she was not going back for her junior year.

I want to be honest about my first reaction, because I think it matters. It was not pure, clear-eyed wisdom. It was a split second of the same collective programming that I had spent years clearing in myself. What about her degree? What about the plan? What will people think? What if she regrets this?

And then something settled. Because I had lived this. I had walked away from a $40,000 paycheck when it stopped being in integrity. I had fired Stanford Cancer Center when my gut said no. I had chosen my knowing over conventional wisdom enough times to understand exactly what it felt like from the inside when that knowing was real. And I recognized it in her voice.

She was not running away from something. She was running toward something. And she had learned that distinction by watching me do it.

Isabella joined the company full-time. She worked hard, accumulated her master certifications, eventually became our Director of Coaching and now trains our certification programs.

She is a part of the executive team and one of the most gifted coaches I have ever watched work, helping people access transformations that traditionally trained therapists often cannot reach, before she is twenty-five years old. The clients who work with her do not care that she does not have a college degree. They care that she can see them clearly and help them change. Which she absolutely can.

Some people thought she was out of her mind. Some thought I was out of my mind for supporting it. Those people are still waiting for the whole thing to fall apart.

And here is the thing I actually want you to take from this story. It is not about Isabella's career. It is not even really about the department head who did not understand emotional intelligence, though that detail is fucking terrifying.

It is about what Isabella watched that made the decision possible. She watched her mother choose her own knowing over institutional authority, over and over and over again. Not recklessly. Not from ego. From a deep, clear, evidence-based trust in what she had seen work with her own eyes. She watched me live in my genius and choose what was best for me, no matter what anyone else said was right or responsible or the way it should be done.

And when her moment came, she already knew what that looked like. She had been watching it her whole life.

My decision to trust myself gave her permission to trust herself. Her courage came from watching mine. Her clients' transformations come from her courage. One ripple. Already three generations deep. And nowhere near finished.

The Man Who Came to Heal and Ended Up Changing the World

George came to us with one goal. He wanted to heal his relationship with his son, whom he had not spoken to in five years. That was it. That was the whole ask. Just get back to his son.

What happened next is one of my favorite examples of what transformation actually looks like when someone commits to doing the real work at the level where it actually lives.

George did the deep unconscious work. He cleared the programs that had been running his behavior for decades, the ones he had been managing and working around and white-knuckling through for most of his adult life. He rebuilt his relationship with his son. He reconnected with his wife, Lynn, in a way he had not thought was possible anymore. He started showing up differently in his law practice. More clients. More speaking engagements. More of the work that actually lit him up.

That was the first ripple.

Then something interesting happened. As George continued to do the internal work, he got clearer, and he started seeing the people around him more clearly, too. He looked at his colleagues in the legal profession and recognized something he had once lived himself: attorneys burning out at an alarming rate, carrying enormous emotional weight with zero tools for processing it, performing strength while privately drowning.

He knew what that cost because he had paid it.

So he built something. George created a specialized lawyer certification program, approved by the American Bar Association, specifically designed to help attorneys avoid burnout through mindset and emotional intelligence work.

He took everything he had learned about the unconscious mind and the four bodies and what it actually means to be a human being doing hard work in a high-stakes environment, and he built it into a framework that is now changing the legal profession.

That was the second ripple.

Then he made a film. He worked with some of the most respected voices in personal development and conscious leadership, people like Joe Vitale and John Assaraf, and he created something specifically about what becomes possible when a person does the real unconscious work. What he had learned working with us was at the center of it. He invited our whole team to the premiere. Standing in that room watching him introduce us to people who had spent their careers in this field, saying everything he had talked about in this film came from us, was one of those moments that remind you exactly why you do this work.

That was the third ripple.

And then, most recently, George was knighted. He is now Baron George, and the work he is doing in the world through philanthropy and leadership and the programs he has built touches thousands of people who will never know his name or ours.

That was the fourth ripple. All in 4 years of working with us. He is still going.

When George first walked through our doors, he was not thinking about changing the legal profession or making films or being knighted. He was thinking about his son. He had one thing he wanted to fix. And because he was willing to go all the way into the real work instead of just managing the surface of it, what came out the other side was something neither of us could have predicted from where he was standing.

That is what transformation actually produces when you stop treating it like a problem to solve and start treating it like a life to expand. The ripple does not end at you. It does not end with the people closest to you. It goes places you cannot see from where you are standing right now, touching people you have never met, changing things you will never personally witness.

George came in wanting to heal. He left with a legacy. And that legacy is still being written.

You Are Already the Spark. Now Become the Fire.

Before you feel too warm about these stories and close the chapter feeling inspired, I need to hand you the part that is actually the most exciting thing in this entire book. Not the most comfortable. The most exciting.

Your current vibration is already creating a ripple effect. Right now. Today. With the version of you that picked up this book, did the work, answered the questions, and sat with the uncomfortable truths. That version of you is already different from the one who opened Chapter 1.

And that difference is already moving through the world, whether you have announced it or not.

Remember entrainment. The people closest to you are not just observing you. They are being influenced by your energetic field, whether they know it or not, and whether you intended it or not. Your kids. Your team. Your friends. Your clients. The stranger who sat next to you on an airplane last Tuesday and walked away feeling inexplicably better about their life. They are all calibrating what is possible based in part on the frequency you are broadcasting.

Not what you say. What you vibrate.

And here is what I need you to really hear: you do not have to be finished to be powerful. You do not have to have the whole thing figured out, every program cleared, every pattern dissolved, every ceiling lifted, before your transformation starts mattering to other people. It matters right now. In the middle of the process.

In the still-figuring-it-out, baby-giraffe-legs, not-quite-solid-yet version of the new you. People can feel the difference between someone who is becoming and someone who is stuck. They can feel the difference between someone who is moving toward something real and someone who is performing contentment while quietly dying inside a life they chose for the wrong reasons.

You are becoming. And that is enough to be the spark.

And here is the distinction I want to make, because there is a difference between being the spark and being the fire. And you are built for both.

The spark is the moment of recognition. The glimpse of what is possible. The person in the room who is vibrating slightly higher than everyone else, and permitting people to consider that maybe they could too. The spark changes the atmosphere. It shifts what feels available. It is powerful and necessary, and it is already what you are.

The fire is what happens when you do the full unconscious work.

When the programs are not just understood but actually cleared. When the identity is not just intended but actually rebuilt from the inside out. When the four bodies are all tended and aligned and working together, instead of the mental body dragging the other three along behind it. When you are not occasionally accessing the expanded frequencies on your good days, but consistently living there as your baseline.

The fire does not just change the atmosphere. It lights other fires. It reaches people you will never personally touch. It creates transformations in people who will never know your name, because the people you transformed went on to transform others, who transformed others, and the ripple went so far out that the original spark is impossible to trace.

George did not know he was going to change the legal profession when he came to us wanting his son back. Isabella did not know she was going to become a head coach when she was sitting in a classroom watching a department head fail to understand emotional intelligence. They were just doing their work. Living their truth. Raising their vibration. Being the fire.

And here is what none of them knew when they started: the fire does not deplete you. That is what most people expect. That living at a higher frequency, that showing up as your full self, that being the person who permits other people to expand, is going to cost you something. Take something from you. Drain something that needs replenishing.

It does not.

Think about a tuning fork. Strike it, and it vibrates at a specific frequency. Hold it near another tuning fork, and that one begins to resonate too, without the first one losing a single bit of its own vibration.

That is entrainment. That is what you are. And here is the part that makes this genuinely extraordinary: energy expressed at a high frequency does not deplete. It expands. It amplifies. It multiplies.

The more people you bring into resonance with your frequency, the stronger your own frequency becomes, not weaker. The more you give from that expanded state, the more of it there is. Sharing your genius does not diminish it. It deepens it. You are not a limited supply. You are a frequency. And frequencies, when they are fully expressed and consistently maintained, do not run out. They reach further.

You are not going to run out.

You were not built to run out.

You were built to be the fire that lights the room and then lights the next room and then the next, carrying your own flame the entire time, burning brighter the further you go, reaching people you will never see and who will feel the warmth of something that started with one person deciding to stop playing small.

So here is what I want to leave you with before we move into the final chapter. Stop waiting until you are finished to start being the fire. The finishing does not come first. The spark comes first. You become the fire in the process of becoming, not at the end of it.

Every step up the vibration scale. Every cleared program. Every moment you choose courage over comfort. Every time you trust your knowing over the noise. Every time you operate from the expanded frequencies instead of the contracted ones.

Each one of those moments is a flame handed to someone watching you.

Your ripple effect is not optional. It never was. The only real choice you have is whether it points the people watching you toward what is possible or keeps them comfortable inside what is familiar.

You did not read this far to keep people comfortable.

Go be the fire.

YOUR RIPPLE EFFECT INVENTORY

Workbook out. No rushed answers. No sanitized version. This is where you reckon honestly with the effect you are currently having on the people around you, and the effect you are capable of having once the unconscious work is done at the level where it actually lives.

PART 1: THE ENTRAINMENT AUDIT

Think about the five people you spend the most time with. For each one, write one honest sentence: when they leave after spending time with you, do you feel more expanded or more contracted? More possible or more limited? Do not write who you want to be. Write what is actually true right now.

What is your dominant vibration when you are with each of them? Are you showing up from flow or from getting by?

And the harder question: whose vibration are you matching that is not serving either of you? Where is entrainment pulling you down instead of you being the spark that lifts?

PART 2: THE PERMISSION AUDIT

You are constantly permitting the people closest to you to do something through your example. Not through what you tell them is possible, but through how you are actually living. What are you currently permitting them to do based on what they observe, not what you say?

What would you want to be giving them permission for? Be specific. Not "to be brave", brave about what, in the way that matters most to the people watching you.

And who in your life has already changed something because of a ripple you created, even a small one? Write their name. Own it. You did that.

PART 3: THE FUTURE RIPPLE

Close your eyes for a moment. Imagine the version of you who has done the full unconscious work. Programs actually cleared, not just understood. Identity actually rebuilt, not just intended. Vibrating in the expanded frequencies consistently, not occasionally. Who does that version ripple toward? How far does it go? Write what you see.

That gap between the ripple you are creating right now and the ripple you are capable of creating is not a verdict. There is no evidence that you have not done enough, worked hard enough, or wanted it badly enough. It is simply the most exciting thing on your entire map right now. Because that gap means there is more.

More frequency available to you. More fire is waiting to be unleashed. More people whose lives are going to change because you decided to stop playing small. More of you is waiting on the other side of the work you have not yet done at the level where it actually lives.

You did not come this far to stay exactly here. You came this far to see exactly this clearly. And now that you can see it, now that you have the map and the tools and the frameworks and the full honest inventory of where you are and where you are capable of going, there is only one thing left to do. The next chapter is about exactly that. And I promise you, it is worth every single page you turned to get here.

CHAPTER 10
Living Unlocked:
Your Daily Practice for Staying Extraordinary

"Tell me, what is it you plan to do with your one wild and precious life?"
– Mary Oliver

You made it!

I do not mean that in the polite, participation-trophy way. I mean it in the actual, genuine, not-everyone-does-this way. You picked up a book that asked you to look at yourself honestly. You did the assignments. You sat with the uncomfortable parts. You kept reading when it got real.

That is not nothing. That is actually everything, because most people stop exactly where you decided to keep going.

So before we talk about what comes next, I want you to stop for a second and actually let that land.

You are not the same person who opened Chapter 1. That person did not have a name for the voice that has been running the show. Did not know about the A-B cycle or how to recognize it while standing inside it. Did not understand why the affirmations were not working or why the vision board produced nothing but a very aesthetically pleasing collection of aspirations. Did not know that 95 percent of everything they thought, felt, and decided was happening without their conscious permission.

You know all of that now. And you cannot unknow it.

Which means this is not the end of something. This is the beginning of everything. And I am genuinely, not-just-saying-this excited for you.

Look How Far You Have Actually Come

Let me show you something. Because I think you have been so deep in the work that you might have missed how much you are actually walking out of these pages with.

You now understand how the unconscious mind works. Not the bumper sticker version. The real version. You know that 95 percent of your behavior is run by programs installed before you had any say in the matter, by people who were doing their best with their own unexamined programs.

You know that your filters are not the truth. They are inherited stories wearing the costume of reality. And you know that the filter can be changed, which means the reality can be changed, which changes everything.

You have the Four Voices framework. You know the difference between your Inner Ego protecting your identity that is no longer serving you, your Inner Critic generating fear dressed up as reason, your Inner Child protecting a wound you may not even remember, and your Intuition, which has been patiently, quietly, unfailingly supporting you and guiding you.

You will never sit in a meeting, have a difficult conversation, or make a major decision the same way again. That distinction lives in you now.

You have the Universal Model of Change. You can see the A-B cycle while you are in it, which is the only way out of it. You know what C actually is, what it requires, and what is waiting on the other side. You know that D is not the end. It is the launchpad. You have the map.

You get to stop being ambushed by your own growth.

You have inteGRITy as a lived practice. You understand that confidence is not a feeling you wait for. It is a track record you build, one kept promise at a time, one decision to honor yourself over what is easier. You understand the difference between an environment that is in integrity and one that quietly erodes your spirit the longer you stay in it.

You understand money as energy. You have the WEALTH framework. You know about the vibration scale and where desire sits and why hustle feels like drowning.

You have Purple Magic Money™ as a manifestation practice and a completely different relationship with what wealth actually means and what it actually provides.

You understand your four bodies and why willpower applied to the mental body, while the other three go untended, produces exactly the results you have been getting. You know what energy work actually does and why it is not supplementary; it is the work. You understand entrainment and ripple effects and the difference between being a spark and being a fire.

That is not a reading list. That is a complete rewiring of how you understand yourself, your patterns, your genius, and your place in the world.

You did that. In ten chapters. While also, presumably, living your life.

That is the genius you were born with.

Playing Big Does Not Look Like What You Think

Here is what nobody tells you about playing big: it is rarely the dramatic, main-stage, three-thousand-person moment. It is rarely the thing you would put on a highlight reel.

It is mostly Tuesdays.

You have the conversation about raising your prices easily and effortlessly, you say the number, you let it land, the other person says yes, and you realize the version of you who just did that without flinching is a completely different human than the one who used to spend three days preparing for a conversation that took three minutes.

It is the email you send because it is exactly what you wanted to say. The idea you share in the meeting because you know it is good. The opportunity you say yes to because your intuition is lit up and you have finally learned to trust that signal over the noise of whether you feel ready. The work you put into the world because it is yours and it is real, and the world genuinely needs it.

It is the truth you hold with warmth and zero drama. The price you raise because you have grown into it, and you know it. The room you walk into as the full version of yourself, not the edited one, not the one sized to fit other people's comfort levels, but the actual one, bringing all of it, unapologetically, because you finally understand that your full presence is a gift and not a problem to manage.

Playing big feels like alignment. It feels like ease. It feels like the specific relief of no longer spending energy on keeping yourself smaller than you are. It feels like moving with instead of against.

Like decisions that used to take a week of anxious deliberation are now being made. Like the right people showing up right when they are supposed to. Like a version of confidence that does not need to perform because it is not borrowed from external validation.

It is built from the inside out, one kept promise at a time, one moment of trusting your knowing over the noise, one ordinary day after another.

And here is the thing about that feeling: it compounds. The first time you show up as the full version, something in you recognizes it as home. The second time, it feels more natural. The third time, you start to forget there was ever another way.

And at some point, with enough repetitions, enough decisions to honor who you actually are over who you thought you were supposed to be, it stops being a choice you make in the moment. It becomes your baseline. Your default. Your frequency.

That is what this whole book has been building toward. Not the one big moment on a stage. The thousand small ordinary moments that add up to a person who lives from their full genius as naturally as they breathe.

You are already becoming that person. You have been since Chapter 1. And she does not need a perfect moment or a perfect setting or anyone's permission to show up exactly as big as she actually is.

She just needs an ordinary Tuesday. And you have one coming tomorrow.

What Going All the Way In Actually Produces

Let me tell you about Shannon, because her story is my favorite answer to the question people always want to ask and rarely say out loud: Is this actually real? Does the work actually produce the life? Or is it just a very compelling set of ideas that sounds great in a book?

Shannon came to us from a corporate job. She was not in crisis. She was not at rock bottom. She was doing fine, which, if you have been paying attention to the last ten chapters, you know, is sometimes the most dangerous place to be. Fine is comfortable enough to stay and unfulfilling enough to quietly hollow you out over time if you let it.

She had two small kids at home and a growing sense that she was missing the time with them that she was never going to get back. She had no particular plan to become a business owner. That was not even on the table. She just knew something needed to shift, and she was willing to do the real work to figure out what.

So she did.

She cleared the programs. She did the unconscious work at the level where it actually lived. She rebuilt her identity around who she actually was instead of who her circumstances had decided she was allowed to be. She raised her vibration from the contracted frequencies of fine and safe and responsible into the expanded frequencies of aligned and purposeful and fully alive, and then she built something.

Four years later, Shannon has generated over two million dollars since leaving her corporate job. She hosts trainings and live events in multiple countries. She has the kind of work and home life balance that most people put on a vision board and quietly stop believing is possible after enough years of not having it. She is present for her kids in the way she always wanted to be. She is building something that matters. She is living in her genius.

Not because she was exceptional when she arrived. Because she was willing to go all the way in when she got here.

Here is the part of Shannon's story I want you to sit with. She did not come to us with a business plan. She did not come to us knowing she was an entrepreneur. She came to us willing. Willing to look at what was running her unconscious mind. Willing to clear what was not serving her. Willing to trust that what was on the other side of the real work was worth whatever it cost to get there.

She had no idea that saying yes to the work would produce a life she had not yet dared to imagine.

And that is exactly the point. You cannot see the other side from where you are currently standing. The programs running your life right now literally cannot compute the version of your life that is available on the other side of clearing them. That is not a limitation. That is the most exciting thing about what comes next.

Shannon did not imagine two million dollars and international events when she first sat down with us. She just said yes to the work. The rest was what happened when the work was actually done.

Living From the Expanded Frequencies: Not a Checklist, a Way of Being

Here is what I am NOT going to do in this section: give you a seven-step morning routine. Hand you a list of things to add to your already full life. Tell you to breathe more, go outside, light a candle, and journal your feelings. You know how to find that advice. It is everywhere. It has probably not changed your life...yet, which is why you are here.

What I want to talk about instead is this: what does it actually feel like to live from the expanded frequencies? Because that is the real goal. Not the practices themselves. The state those practices produce. The frequency. The way of being. And once you know what that feels like in your body, you will stop needing a checklist to get there. You will just know when you are there and when you are not. And you will know exactly what to do about it.

Living from the expanded frequencies feels like ease. Like moving with instead of against. Like the version of effort that does not deplete you because it is coming from alignment rather than friction.

You will recognize it because decisions that used to take a week of deliberation will start making themselves. Opportunities that used to feel overwhelming will start feeling like obvious yeses. The right people will keep showing up right when they are supposed to.

Not because you manifested harder. Because you got out of your own way.

It also does not feel like constant bliss, so let's not romanticize this. Life still "life-s." Difficult things still happen. The difference is in how you meet them. From the contracted frequencies, a hard thing feels like proof that everything is falling apart.

From the expanded frequencies, a hard thing feels like information. Like the universe clearing its throat about something that needs attention. Like a course correction rather than a catastrophe. The emotional charge is completely different. The recovery time is completely different.

The story you tell yourself about it is completely different.

And here is the part that ties all four bodies together in a way no checklist ever could: when you are consistently doing the unconscious work, the energy work, the somatic work, the spiritual practice that tends the fourth body, you start to develop a felt sense of your own frequency.

You know when you are in flow and when you have slipped. You know it in your body before your mind catches up. And that knowing is its own kind of intelligence. The kind that no framework can fully give you and no book can fully install. It has to be lived.

What I want for you is a life where your baseline is the expanded state. Where flow is your normal, not your occasional good day. Where you are operating from the full expression of all four bodies consistently, not grinding through the week and then recovering on the weekend.

Where the practices are not the things you do to compensate for how depleted you are. They are the things you do because you genuinely, enthusiastically love the version of yourself they connect you to.

That version is not a future project. She is available right now. She has always been available. You just needed the map, the tools, and the willingness to go deeper than the surface.

You have all three.

The Gap Is Not a Problem. It Is a Preview.

I want to talk about the gap one more time before we close. Not the gap between where you are and where you think you should be. The gap between where you are right now and what becomes possible when you do the next level of the work.

The awareness you have built in these pages is genuinely transformational. And it is also the first layer. The entry point. The thing that makes everything underneath it accessible in a way it was not before.

The people who get the results that look impossible from the outside are not more gifted than you. They are not more disciplined, more motivated, or more deserving of the transformation.

They are simply the ones who went deeper. Who did not stop at understanding the pattern and went all the way to clearing it. Who did not stop at naming the program and went all the way to actually replacing it. Who did not stop at the map and went all the way into the territory.

And here is the thing about going deeper that nobody tells you until you are on the other side of it: it is not harder than staying where you are. It is actually easier.

Because staying where you are, managing the patterns, white-knuckling through the ceiling, spinning in the A-B cycle with excellent vocabulary about why you are spinning, that is the hard thing. That is what exhausting looks like. Going through the C, doing the real unconscious work, clearing what is actually running the show, that is the thing that ends the exhaustion.

The gap between where you are and where you get to be is not a gap of effort. It is a gap of depth. And depth is not something you force. It is something you choose.

With support. With the right tools. With someone who can see the label on your jar and help you clear what is inside it at the level where it actually lives.

You have spent ten chapters learning that you cannot read the label from inside the jar. You know that now. You have felt it in the moments this book landed on something true that you could not quite access on your own before.

That is not the limit of what is available. That is just the beginning of what becomes possible when someone is standing on the outside of the jar, seeing the label clearly, and finally telling you what it says.

That is what we do. And if any part of you just felt a pull when you read that, your intuition is doing exactly what it is supposed to do.

Trust it.

Your Genius Has Always Been Real

Do you remember Chapter 1? The astronomical odds of your existence. The one in ten-to-the-power-of-two-point-five-million-zeros probability that you would be here at all. The fact that you beat the most impossible odds in the history of the universe before you took your first breath.

You were not born for mediocrity. You were not born to spend your life managing the surface of things, running old programs that were never yours to begin with, vibrating at frequencies installed by people who were doing their own version of the same thing. You were not born to play small or stay quiet or make yourself easier to be around at the expense of being fully yourself.

You were born for *this*. For the work of becoming who you actually are, underneath all of it. For the joy of discovering that who you actually are is so much more extraordinary than the version you have been presenting to the world.

For the experience of living from your genius instead of managing the gap between your genius and the version of yourself you thought you were allowed to be.

Every chapter of this book was a step toward that. Toward the truth of you. Toward the version that has been there the entire time, waiting with remarkable patience for you to stop arguing for your limitations and start living from your actual power.

You are not a project to be completed. You are a genius to be unleashed. And the unleashing does not happen once, and then it is done. It is a spiral, exactly like the model in Chapter 5. Each cycle brings you closer to the full expression.

Each A' is the new A, and the seed that lands at the top of the spiral is landing somewhere unimaginably higher than where the last one landed. This is not a destination. It is a direction. And you now know how to keep choosing it.

This book was always meant to be the beginning of a conversation. The most important conversation you will ever have is the one you are about to have with the deepest levels of your own unconscious mind, with proper support, at the depth where the patterns actually live and where everything you have ever wanted is patiently, absolutely, definitely waiting.

You came here because something in you knew you were capable of more. That something was your intuition. It has been right about you this entire time. Every 3 am restlessness. Every moment of looking at your life and knowing in your body that something more is available. Every time you read something in these pages, and had to put the book down because it lands somewhere too real to keep reading.

That was not anxiety. That was not wishful thinking. That was your genius, knocking.

Open the door.

geniusunlocked.coach

YOUR GENIUS UNLEASHED

This is the last assignment in the book. And it is nothing like any of the ones that came before it. No auditing what is broken. No cataloging the patterns. No measuring the gap. You have done all of that. You have been honest about where you are and what it has cost you, and what is ready to change. That work is done.

This assignment is about what comes next. The vision. The inspired action. The version of your life you are now equipped to actually build. Workbook out. Pen ready.

PART 1: THE DECLARATION

You are not the same person who opened Chapter 1. Write who you are now. Not who you are becoming. Who you are, right now, having done this work. What do you know about yourself that you did not know before? What has shifted in how you see yourself? What are you no longer willing to pretend?

What is the most important thing this book cracked open for you? Not a concept. A truth. The one that landed hardest and is still sitting with you.

PART 2: THE VISION

It is one year from today. You have been living everything in this book. Not perfectly. Not without stumbling. Just consistently, from the inside out, at the level where it actually lives. What is different? Be specific. Not "I am more confident," but what does that confidence look like on a Tuesday morning? Not "I am making more money" but how much, doing what, feeling how.

What does your average day feel like in this version of your life? What are you doing, creating, building? Who are you doing it with? What frequency are you living in?

What is the ripple you are creating one year from now? Who has been changed by the version of you who stopped playing small?

PART 3: THE INSPIRED ACTION

Vision without action is just a very detailed daydream. What are the three most important actions you are committing to take in the next thirty days based on everything you now know? Not the safe ones. The real ones. The ones your intuition already knows.

Inspired action 1:

Inspired action 2:

Inspired action 3:

What is the one thing that, if you did it in the next week, would create the most momentum toward the life you described in Part 2? Write it. Then go do it.

PART 4: THE LETTER FROM YOUR FUTURE SELF

This is the one. Write a letter from the version of you living the life in Part 2, one year from today, back to the version of you sitting here right now. What does she want you to know? What does she wish you would stop being afraid of? What does she wish you would trust? What is she most grateful for that you decided to do?

Write it in her voice. Let her be as certain as she actually is. Let her be big. She has been waiting to speak.

Everything in this book has been pointing at one thing. Not a framework. Not a strategy. Not a cleverly named acronym, a morning routine, or a better relationship with your limiting beliefs. Not even the unconscious mind, as extraordinary as that piece is. It's been pointing at…

You.

The full, unedited, completely unapologetic, absolutely extraordinary version of you that has been underneath all of it this entire time. The one that existed before the programs got installed and the filters got built, and you learned to make yourself smaller to fit inside spaces that were never designed to hold all of you.

The one that was there before you decided that wanting more made you ungrateful, and trusting yourself was arrogant, and playing big was something that happened to other people who were somehow more qualified for it than you were.

That version of you did not go anywhere while all of that was happening. She has been here the entire time. Waiting with the kind of patience that only comes from knowing, absolutely and without question, that her moment was going to come.

You opened this book because something in you knew.

You finished it for the same reason.

That something has never once been wrong about you. Not when it whispered at 3 am that more was possible. Not when it made you uncomfortable inside a life that looked fine from the outside. Not when it kept landing in your chest every time something in these pages hit too close to the truth to be a coincidence.

That was not anxiety. That was not wishful thinking. That was the most trustworthy voice you have ever had access to, pointing you exactly here, to this moment, to this page, to this version of yourself that is standing on the other side of ten chapters of the most honest work most people never do.

She is done waiting.

And here is what I need you to hear before you close this book. You are not at the end of something. You are at the beginning of everything. The real work, the deep work, the work that clears the patterns at the root and rebuilds the identity from the inside out and opens up the version of your life that the current you cannot fully picture yet, that work is what comes next.

And you are more ready for it than you have ever been, not because you finished a book, because you finally understand what has actually been running the show. You have the map. You have the language. You have the awareness that makes the next level of work possible in a way that it was not possible before you opened Chapter 1.

Shannon did not know what was waiting for her. George did not know. Isabella did not know. None of the people in these pages could see from where they were standing what was available on the other side of going all the way in.

Neither can you. And that is the most thrilling thing about where you are standing right now.

You were always this. Every single page of this book was just the beginning of the work of clearing everything that was in the way of you finally being able to see it.

You have always, always been exactly this ready. You Are Worth It!

Now go show them.

RESOURCES

Workbook

Meditation

About the Author

Jenn Noble-Beninger is the founder and CEO of Genius Unlocked, and she has a confession to make: she spent years playing it safe, playing it small, and playing by everyone else's rules. Spoiler alert…it didn't work. What *did* work? Blowing the whole thing up and rebuilding from the inside out.

Today, Jenn is one of only 150 Internationally Accredited Master Certified NLP Trainers on the planet (yes, the entire planet), holds 16 master-level, internationally recognized certifications, and has helped thousands of people stop shrinking and start *living*. She scaled Genius Unlocked from $7,000 to over $7 million, including a jaw-dropping $1 million in revenue through referrals alone during a pandemic, when the rest of the world was panic-buying toilet paper.

Her résumé reads like someone couldn't decide between corporate titan and spiritual revolutionary, so she became both. She was in the rooms where WebMD went public and helped shape strategy at a billion-dollar company. She holds a B.S. in Psychology, has been featured on NBC, ABC, CBS, USA Today, and the LA Tribune, received the Presidential Lifetime Achievement Award, and was knighted by the Royal Order of Constantine the Great and Saint Helen and the Principality of Cappadocia — yes, *knighted* — earning the title of Dame Jenn Noble-Beninger. Apparently, rewiring unconscious minds at scale is the kind of thing that gets you noticed by royalty. She is also a three-time Amazon bestselling author. Basically, she's an overachiever, but the fun kind.

Here's what the fancy credentials don't tell you: Jenn has survived burnout, breast cancer, business betrayal, and oh yeah, a divorce. She didn't just survive them; she used them as fuel. Because that's what happens when you stop playing small. The hard stuff stops being the end of your story and starts becoming the *beginning* of your best one.

When she's not rewiring unconscious minds or speaking on stages around the world, you'll find her skydiving (yes, on purpose), leading transformational retreats in places from Belize to Bali, or raising two brilliant adult daughters in Northern California while definitely drinking really good coffee, describing and plotting world domination, the benevolent kind.

Jenn doesn't teach you to think differently. She rewires how your unconscious mind operates. And if that sounds like exactly what you need right now, well... you're holding the right book written by the right person to help you thrive.

READY TO GO DEEPER?

You made it to the end of this book. That means something has shifted; you feel it. You've also probably noticed some of the stuff that came up while you were reading? It didn't just dissolve because you had an insight about it. That's not how transformation actually works.

Reading about the stages of change is powerful. ***Doing*** the work to release the emotional charge behind the stories, the fear, the patterns that built the cage you've been living in? That's a different level entirely.

That's what **Activate** is for.

Activate is Genius Unlocked's signature certification experience, a three-part live event where you'll work directly alongside Jenn and her team of master-level coaches who will guide you through your own real, live breakthrough.

Actual release work at the core level, in a container built to hold you while you become someone new.

Using the science-backed tools of Neuro Linguistic Programming (NLP), Quantum Release Process, Professional Coaching, Somatic and Energy work, you'll leave with three internationally recognized certifications and, more importantly, the lived experience of what it actually feels like to be free of the thing that's been running the show.

The difference between reading about change and being ***in the room*** with people who've dedicated their lives to creating it?

You'll feel it in your bones by day two.

This is the jetpack. The trampoline. The part where the book stops being something you read and starts being someone you ***are.***

Come find out what's waiting for you on the other side.

GeniusUnlocked.Coach/Activate

Come Fully Unlock Your Genius - You Are Worth It!

Made in the USA
Las Vegas, NV
09 August 2026

52660380R00115